LIGHT RAIL REVIEW

CONTENTS

Published by the Light Rail Transit Association and Platform 5 Publishing Ltd.

Edited by Michael Taplin and Peter Fox.

ISBN 1 872524 00 1

Printed by Amadeus Press, 517 Leeds Road, Huddersfield; Maxwell Data Management, Slack Lane, Derby and Icon Impressions, Yorkshire Street, Bacup, Lancs.

Further copies of this publication may be obtained from Platform 5 Publishing Ltd. or the Light Rail Transit Association at the above addresses, price £6.95. Please add 10% (UK) 20% (overseas) to cover postage and packing.

FOREWORD by Dr Tony M. Ridley CBE, FCIT, FICE

Managing Director – Project, Eurotunnel; President of the Light Rail Transit Association

I am delighted to introduce this Light Rail Review, which has been produced to co-incide with the major international conference 'Light Rail 89' in Bristol and the 52nd Annual General Meeting of the Association of which I have the honour to be President. Fifteen Years ago, when I was Director-General of the then Tyneside Passenger Transport Executive, I welcomed LRTA members to Newcastle. They were in that city to hear about plans for an integrated public transport system on Tyneside, a system with light rail trains running on rejuvenated railway alignments, linked by city centre tunnels as its backbone.

That system was built with central government funding in recognition of its regional importance, and had enormous success is stimulating mobility and helping the area's economic recovery. Times and governments have changed. In Great Britain integration and local authority control have given way to deregulation, competition and privatisation. Yet today there are light rail proposals in over a dozen British cities, and in Manchester they are now following Newcastle's lead in pulling together a regional railway system with access through the city centre. The crucial difference in Manchester, as indeed with the plans for Bristol, is that this access will be achieved on the streets, using the inherent flexibility of light rail to achieve visible, high quality, cost-effective transport.

Transport studies carried out in Tyneside, London Docklands, Manchester, Sheffield, Bristol and Birmingham have shown that light rail is the basis for an effective way of dealing with their common problems of urban mobility and urban regeneration, and as 'green' issues assume increasing importance, a healthier environment. Effective means both cost-effective and capable of implementation. There has always been a shortage of finance for urban transport projects, and those that offer the best cost:benefit ratio and the best prospects of attracting private capital are those most likely to win approval. Light rail demands much less capital than expensive tunnels, or unsightly overhead structures, yet can bring the prosperity that the visible permanence of a railway always promotes, and good accessibility brings more passengers.

As I write rails are being laid in the streets of Los Angeles. That should tell you something about cities that try to cope with personal mobility by giving the private car free rein. Los Angeles is the eighth North American city to build a light rail system in the last 12 years, and several more are in the pipeline. I do not advocate light rail in every situation, yet it can be more efficient than buses on their own, and will always be less costly than heavy rail solutions.

The pages of this review, and the Association's monthly magazine "Modern Tramway" will bring you up to date with the latest developments and show you what is being achieved. The next decade will be exciting indeed.

Editorial

There are two ways of looking at a new transport system. The first is as a purely commercial enterprise. If the total revenue is enough to meet all capital and operating costs, plus a working profit, then the system is worth building.

The second way is to look at the benefits the system brings to the community as a whole. These may include benefits to the users, such as reduced journey times or improved comfort, and benefits to non-users, such as reduced congestion, or reductions in noise levels or air pollution. These are very real factors, but they do not appear on the transport operator's balance sheet. If all these other benefits are taken into account, then a project which may not be worthwhile in purely financial terms may still be a very good investment for the economy of the area it serves.

Any new highway scheme has to be justified solely in terms of the benefits it is estimated to bring, since in the absence of road pricing, there is no revenue from the users. But a new public transport scheme is regarded very differently, at least in the UK. To qualify for government grant any new scheme has to meet rigorous criteria set by the Department of Transport (DTp) and Treasury. Unlike highway schemes, user-benefits are not allowed to be included, on the grounds that any real benefits will be reflected in higher fares and hence increased revenue. The DTp approach is decidedly non user-friendly.

And yet any reader of Modern Tramway magazine can explain that light rail transit is distinctly user-friendly. It is probably the most comfortable, attractive, speedy, reliable and efficient mode of urban transport for everyday journeys. That is why it is being built in cities as diverse as San Jose, Istanbul and Manchester.

But light rail is also non-user friendly. It relieves congestion and thus helps those who do not actually travel on it. Its environmental qualities enable a whole new way of life in crowded city streets, free from car noise and fumes, as the citizens of Grenoble and Portland have recently discovered.

The DTp does recognise that congestion costs and benefits should be included in evaluation processes, although how actually to measure them remains something of a mystery. But unless all the benefits that light rail can bring, to both users and non-users, are taken fully into account, then many promising schemes for light rail in British towns and cities may never leave the drawing board. And that would be very short-sighted at a time when urban congestion is growing relentlessly, and Britain needs light rail more than at any period in the past.

A recent survey by the Confederation of British Industry estimates that the cost to businesses of traffic congestion is £15 000 million per annum. This is a staggering sum and shows only too dramatically just how serious the urban transport crisis has become in Britain. The cost of providing every large and medium-sized city with a light rail system would be modest by comparison.

The government expects that any new system should be funded largely by the private sector, although some grants under Section 56 of the 1968 Transport Act may be available where the demanding criteria can be met.It is reasonable to expect private funding where there are profits to be made, either by translating user benefits into revenue, or perhaps from non-user benefits such as the increase in development land values. But it is wholly unreasonable to expect the private sector to provide the capital when the bulk of the benefits are to the community as a whole. That is why France has its payroll tax (versement transport), West Germany has its extra fuel tax, and the United States has both sales and fuel taxes, to help fund public transport investment. Britain desperately needs a comparable source of funds.

Another issue of concern also relates to non-users, and that is noise. Anyone who has travelled on a modern light rail system will know that noise levels are extremely low, especially when compared with a conventional bus or train. But the House of Lords Select Committee on the Bill dealing with the Docklands Light Railway extension to Beckton has imposed a maximum noise level of 65 dB(A) (24 hr LEQ) beyond which noise insulation will require to be paid for. This could increase the cost of the scheme by a very substantial sum.

And yet comparable criteria for highway schemes require a level of 70 dB(A) before insulation must be provided. The implications are worrying not just for the DLR, but for London Underground, British Rail and every planned light rail scheme. The resolution of the DLR's specific local noise problems must not be allowed to determine national standards applicable in every situation.

Light rail is ready to play its part in breathing new life into Britain's congested cities, as it has been doing throughout Europe, in Canada, and in the USA and beyond. The 1990s could be a promising an exciting time. But light rail is unlikely to succeed with both financial hands tied behind its back.

EDITOR'S NOTE

This editorial is an edited version of that which appeared in Modern Tramway for July 1989. A brief note of explanation may help those whose first language is not English understand the significance of the hyphenation used in places. Non user-friendly means "not friendly to users", while non-user friendly means "friendly to non users".

A ride on Basel's suburban light rail lines will show the community benefit of a modern and efficient system. *J.C. Baker*

MIDLAND METRO

Light Rail Transit for the West Midlands

by Michael Ballinger

BACKGROUND

The West Midlands Passenger Transport Authority's proposed light rail scheme, launched in September 1987, is the largest such project under consideration in the United Kingdom. The area of the former metropolitan county, now administered by the seven district councils of Birmingham, Coventry, Dudley, Sandwell, Solihull, Walsall and Wolverhampton, is currently engaged on a number of initiatives aimed at regenerating the local economy, which suffered considerable decline in the recent recession.

TRANSPORTATION

To spur redevelopment it was recognised that good transport links are essential, and while external links are much better and at present undergoing further improvement, the local transport system suffered from a lack of balanced investment. In the Black Country much of the infrastructure dates back to the last century, whilst Birmingham's investment in roads in the last two decades has failed to create enough capacity, and restricted the growth of the city centre.

After deregulation in 1986, public transport is operated by a number of private bus companies and by British Rail providing local services through agreement with the PTE. Despite increased competition, bus patronage has declined by some 10%, and the threatened splitting-up of the largest operator, West Midlands Travel, could lead to a less comprehensive network. On the other hand, rail patronage is on the increase and schemes are in progress to modernise the rolling stock and electrify the cross-city line. New stations have been opened, the city-centre terminus at Snow Hill reopened, and in April 1989 passenger services between Walsall and Hednesford were restored 24 years after closure under the Beeching axe. Future developments include the diversion of the Stourbridge line into the refurbished Snow Hill to relieve pressure on the main New Street station.

Successful as it is, development of the conventional rail network is limited by economic and geographical considerations; the seven local lines are all radial to Birmingham city centre with sub-optimal alignments in relation to potential redevelopment areas. In 1982 the County Structure Plan Review proposed the development of a rapid transit system to stem the overall decline in public transport usage, whilst also acting as a catalyst in the regeneration of the area. This led to a study proposing a light rail system, but plans for the first route failed in 1985 through lack of political and public support.

CHOICE OF MODE

As part of the evaluation of the former County Council scheme, studies were made of a variety of types of rapid transit. Heavy systems were discounted because the comparatively low density of development produced passenger flow forecasts by route that could not justify the high level of investment these expensive systems would have required.

An extensive examination of three modes: busways, conventional light rail transit (LRT) and automated guideway systems was undertaken, while the PTE gained practical experience of guided bus operation on a short experimental section of route in Birmingham. In overall terms, conventional LRT was shown to be less expensive than automated guideway systems, whilst still having the positive image of a rail-based system. Experience in Europe and North America has shown that LRT is cheaper to operate than comparable bus-only systems, though it must be stressed that a rapid transit system is seen as being complementary to the existing bus and rail networks.

The main benefits foreseen from a light rail system, as set out in the PTE's three-year plan for 1989–92, are:

(i) it will stimulate regeneration of the region by encouraging increased economic activity, enhancing existing development and initiating new development opportunities through the promotion of business confidence;
(ii) it will improve public transport effectiveness and reverse its decline by the provision of a transport system which is efficient, safe, reliable and attractive and which achieves a high degree of integration with other modes;
(iii) it will assist the mobility of public transport dependent and socially disadvantaged groups, particularly in improving accessibility to social and employment opportunities;
(iv) it will make more effective use of road space by encouraging modal change towards public transport and thereby reducing highway congestion, traffic noise and air pollution;
(v) it will assist in improvement of the environment through the above benefits and provide new opportunities for physical change.

SYSTEM CONCEPT

The LRT system will operate on segregated alignments where possible, to avoid road congestion and ensure fast and consistent journey times. However highway alignments shared with other traffic will be used where no alternative exists or to provide better access to a traffic objective. The light rail vehicles (LRV) will be powered from overhead wires and the system will be designed for two cars to operate in multiple as required. An important feature will be level boarding, making the system easily accessible to mobility-impaired persons; this will be achieved by using vehicles with doors and the majority of the interior floor level about 350mm above rail level, with matching platforms.

CONCEPTION AND BIRTH

Following the formation of the West Midlands Passenger Transport Authority in 1986, a reappraisal of rapid transit was undertaken and the various district councils asked for their views. From this feedback the planners identified a number of routes radiating out of Birmingham and also extending through the Black Country to link the major urban centres. A further examination is being made of a physically-separate, but technically-similar system based on Coventry.

Midland Metro was launched as a project in September 1987, with strong local support across the political spectrum.

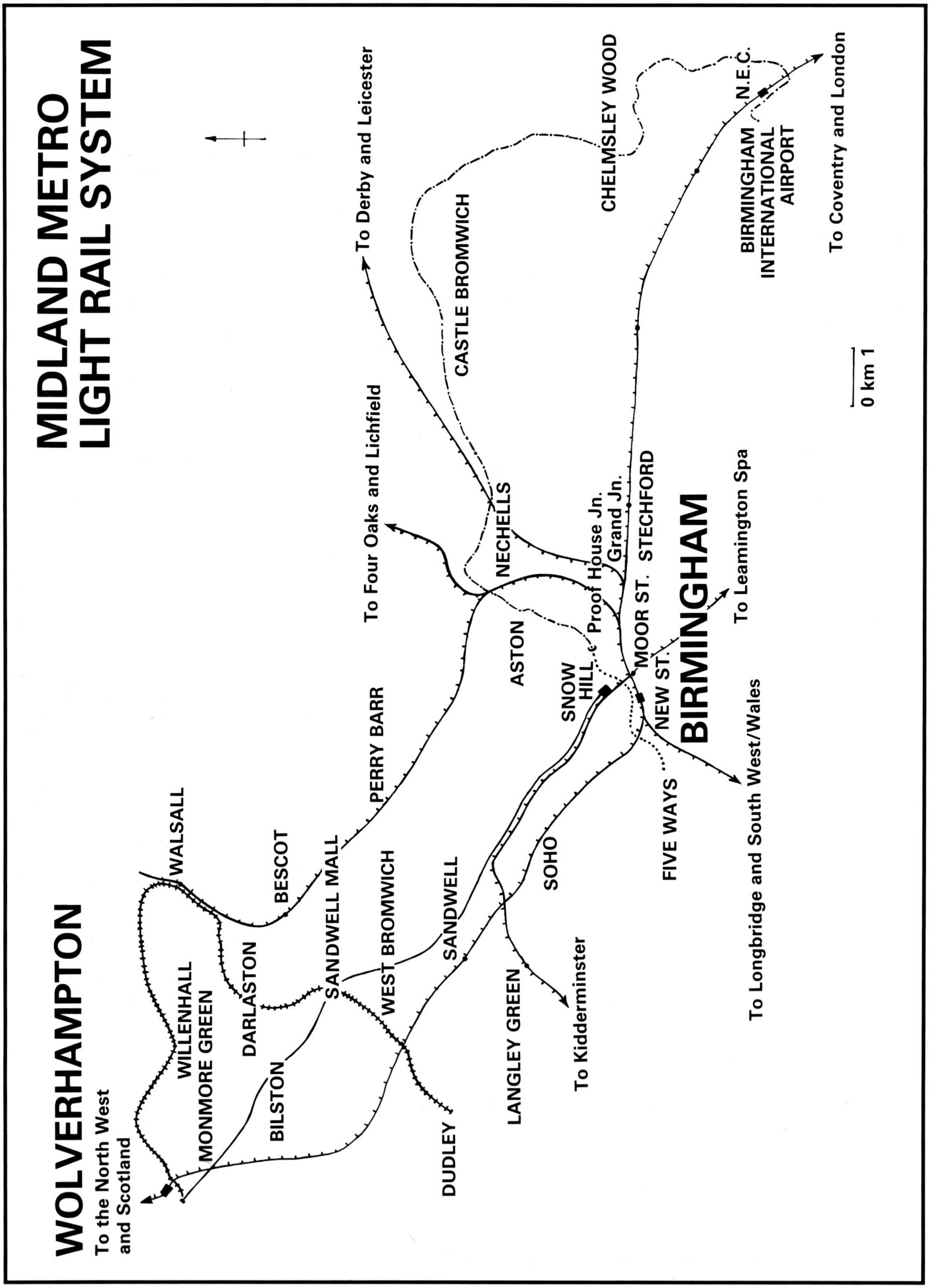

MIDLAND METRO
LIGHT RAIL SYSTEM
WOLVERHAMPTON
To the North West and Scotland
MONMORE GREEN
WILLENHALL
WALSALL
BILSTON
DARLASTON
BESCOT
SANDWELL MALL
WEST BROMWICH
DUDLEY
PERRY BARR
SANDWELL
LANGLEY GREEN
To Kidderminster
SOHO
ASTON
SNOW HILL
To Four Oaks and Lichfield
NECHELLS
Proof House Jn.
Grand Jn.
MOOR ST.
NEW ST.
FIVE WAYS
STECHFORD
BIRMINGHAM
To Longbridge and South West/Wales
To Leamington Spa
To Derby and Leicester
CASTLE BROMWICH
CHELMSLEY WOOD
N.E.C.
BIRMINGHAM INTERNATIONAL AIRPORT
To Coventry and London
0 km 1

Costs were estimated as £200 million for the initial five-year scheme and £800 million for the complete route network, with investment of £25 million per year for 25 years. Potential funding was identified as the European Regional Development Fund, Government grant under section 56 of the 1968 Transport Act, and private sector funding and loans. In February 1988 the first route was identified as Birmingham to Wolverhampton and costed at £65 million. An authorising Bill was lodged in Parliament in November 1988 and made rapid progress through both Houses, so that Royal Assent was expected in October 1989. If all goes well the first car will run in 1993.

THE FIRST ROUTE

The 20-km line linking Birmingham and Wolverhampton will start from platform 4 of Snow Hill station and follow the abandoned railway (former Great Western Railway) alignment for all but the last two kilometres. In order to penetrate Wolverhampton town centre more effectively, the line will transfer at Monmore Green to a shared highway alignment along the centre of Bilston Road, moving to a central reservation near Sharrocks Street. After crossing the ring road under traffic signal control, the line reaches its initial terminus in the southern carriageway of Bilston Street.

The route will serve West Bromwich, Wednesbury and Bilston, areas ripe for redevelopment with 300 acres available for industry, 140 acres for housing and 80 acres for mixed retail and leisure projects, all within one kilometre of the line. Lest one should think that the line will run through a virtual desert, there are also over 130 000 people living within the same area, where unemployment is still significant (two in three households do not have access to employment).

The depot will be built at Wednesbury, between Leabrook Road and the Walsall–Dudley freight line (the latter also a possible future LRT alignment). This is an ideal site for delivery of rolling stock by rail and subsequent operations (it is near the mid-point of the line), with room for expansion as necessary.

FUTURE PLANS

In 1988 the PTE commissioned a detailed study to evaluate key traffic corridors in terms of revenue and economic regeneration potential, ease of construction and environmental impact. The study supported line 1 then before Parliament, and identified further routes for priority consideration. Again the district councils were approached for their views and all the selected corridors were approved by the relevant authorities for further investigation leading to detailed route proposals.

In terms of feasibility for submission of a further Bill to Parliament in November 1989, three routes were selected:

Wolverhampton–Willenhall–Walsall;
Walsall–Darlaston–Wednesbury–Dudley;
Birmingham–Chelmsley Wood–National Exhibition Centre–Airport.

The first two routes are based on disused or freight-only railways, although LRT and freight operations would always be segregated. However in Wolverhampton street operation would again be used to run through areas that are due for redevelopment and also to serve the New Cross hospital complex. There would also be a short section of street track to take the Walsall–Wednesbury line under the M6 motorway, and another to penetrate Dudley town centre.

The 20 km route proposed by the City of Birmingham and Borough of Solihull will link Five Ways in Birmingham, the new International Convention Centre now under construction, New Street station, the Birmingham Heartlands development area, Chelmsley Wood and the NEC and Airport complex. A number of alternative alignments were evaluated, but the main decision to be made was the choice between subway and surface running in Birmingham city centre. After much discussion it was decided that the underground option provided the best long-term benefit and avoided major strategic decisions about the future of the car in the main shopping area. The difference in cost for the line with subway compared with on surface is £238 million to £210 million, a relatively small difference accounted for by the likely effect on the commercial speed and hence the productivity of a surface alignment through the central street complex, and topography.

All the detailed routes were put out to extensive, and sometimes heated, consultation, and were confirmed in July 1989 so that work on the November Bill submission could go ahead.

Future possibilities (apart from the Coventry network already mentioned) include further radial routes around Birmingham, a link from the NEC to Solihull, and more Black Country routes. In the latter category a line between Dudley and West Bromwich via Oldbury and Sandwell & Dudley rail station is a high priority, as this would give a connection from the InterCity network to the various tourist attractions that are being developed in Dudley.

In 1893 one of Britain's first electric tramways to be powered from an overhead wire was opened in Wednesbury. Hopefully 1993 will see the opening of the first stage of the much-needed light rail system that should revolutionise travel in the same way that the coming of the tramways did at the turn of the century. There is much to be achieved before that happens, but the prospects for Midland Metro are improving rapidly.

KEY FOR MIDLAND METRO MAP ON PAGE 4

BRITISH RAIL

MIDLAND METRO AUTHORISED
(LOW LEVEL LINE: BILSTON STREET WOLVERHAMPTON TO SNOW HILL BIRMINGHAM)

MIDLAND METRO PROPOSED
(LINE 2: FIVE WAYS TO BIRMINGHAM AIRPORT)

MIDLAND METRO PROPOSED
LINE 3: WOLVERHAMPTON, WALSALL, DUDLEY)

CONFERENCE REPORT

Light Rail Transit: Funding and Implementation 1989

by Jack Wyse

On 24th May, the Transport Unit of the Civil Engineering Department of Aston University, Birmingham arranged a one-day conference entitled 'Light Rail Transit: Funding and Implementation 1989', attended by some 110 delegates. The Chairman was Paul Truelove of the Transport Unit.

PAPER 1: METHODS OF ASSESSING SECTION 56 GRANT APPLICATIONS

by Tom Worlsey, Senior Economic Adviser of the Department of Transport (DTp).

The paper was of great interest to many delegates. Mr Worsley first gave the background role of 'pricing and fare policy' in determining public transport provision. The farebox revenue was the main source for meeting running costs and system-specific costs, and the demand at that level in the open market indicated the funding required. The approach was inevitably politically-influenced, and government thinking was that too low a fare would generate additional demand which required more capacity, but failed to fund the extra investment needed to provide that extra capacity. Such provision took much time; even London Underground (LUL) needed 5–6 years to increase tube capacity by resignalling, while a new tube line needed 10 years. The conclusion was that the only short-term option was to use prices to control demand and investment.

His second topic was 'Recent trends in subsidy and regulation of public transport'. Growth in demand for rail services, especially in the Network SouthEast (NSE) area, apparently reduced the need for subsidy because revenue increased more rapidly than costs, but concealed the fact that the subsidy was used to maintain existing service rather than invest in extra capacity, the DTp having made it clear that it would not countenance closures. As a consequence, both NSE and Provincial sectors desperately needed new rolling stock. When NSE passenger numbers increased in 1983, it signified a real trend but was mistaken for a 'blip'. The initial response to coach deregulation was 30% more passengers and 40% lower fares and, to the pleasure of DTp, BR responded by fare-cutting. This eliminated the rationale for Intercity subsidy, and IC services now made a small profit. For local buses, subsidy came from local authorities, often concession-fare based; deregulation in October 1986 had controversial consequences, but generally had reduced operating costs and subsidies.

Turning more specifically to Section 56 Grants, these had originated when the Commons Transport Committee studied the financing of rail services, and in 1986 they had questioned why any subsidy was paid. The government had published a considered response to the Committee reports for 1985–7 and said that grants should be related to measurable objectives. Their aim was to reduce the burden on taxpayers and transfer costs to users, based on the political philosophy that subsidies led to inefficient operation. Mr Worsley pointed out that the government had initiated no significant rail closures, even allowing the Settle–Carlisle line to continue in operation, whilst insisting that taxpayers should not help to keep fares down. This response applied firstly to heavy railways but it was also felt valid for application to buses, light rail and so on. Changes in 1985 made Transport Supplementary Grant no longer available for many projects, including those for London Transport and BR. Consultations on the draft guidelines were now almost complete, and the final Guidance Note was due in summer/autumn 1989.

After this introduction, Mr Worsley turned to project appraisal. The first step was to identify the base case and the options for consideration. This included what would happen if the project did not go ahead; where rail services were involved, the costs and benefits of closure had to be found; then there were minimum-cost options such as traffic management, pricing policy to change demand; finally, for an LRT scheme, the core investment and incremental options had to be worked out.

The second step was to list and quantify passenger benefits. Demand forecasts had to take account of improved service quality; effect of various fare structure changes such as higher fares at peak times on willingness to pay – research was needed into passenger reactions with new transport modes; and the reactions of other operators – here, for light rail, it was important to distinguish between bus competition and feeding.

The third step was to estimate project costs, including sensitivity-testing on capital and operating costs, and cost changes elsewhere, including the knock-on effect on BR.

The fourth step was to compare the net present value of costs and revenues. Here, if revenues exceeded costs, capital allocation was likely to be sanctioned from whatever source was appropriate; otherwise, a grant application would proceed. In this situation, the scope for funding from developers would be explored; if, after this, revenues were still below costs, the next consideration would be the scope for global or selective fare increases, and the scope for grant in e.g. reduction in road congestion.

With a grant still required, the fifth step would be to quantify road decongestion benefits using traffic-modelling techniques. In a congested road network with latent traffic to take the place of that creamed-off by LRT, iterations would have to continue until convergent results appeared. A point of interest was that new users of roads were considered as getting benefits which could be quantified, and added to other benefits.

For a 'pump-priming' development, assumptions would have to be made on fares, but increases should not encourage a user's monopoly power, i.e. they should not exceed user-benefits. This involved putting a value on users' time, as in cost/benefit analysis, and making allowance for people's own perception of the value of their time.

An interesting point was raised in the discussion on how the benefits would be worked out in a road-pricing situation when LRT weaned motorists from their cars. To this very tricky question, Mr Worsley replied that it would depend on "the shape of the curves", a tactful reply which satisfied those of the audience (like your reporter) who didn't have a clue either!

PAPER 2: METROLINK MANCHESTER: CONTRACT DOCUMENTATION AND PROJECT APPRAISAL
by Roger Hall, Project Executive of GMPTE.

Mr Hall outlined the development of the project and felt that Metrolink would be the guinea-pig for DTp to assess private involvement in the operation of an LRT system. Manchester's first submission for a Section 56 Grant had been in 1985, and in 1987–8 the DTp wanted more allowance made for deregulation; both DTp and Greater Manchester (GM) engaged merchant bankers to bring in private sector options and to see what degree of privatisation might be possible. GM favoured full public involvement, an approach rejected by DTp, who favoured the complete concession approach in which all the assets remained in PTE ownership but where the private sector would bid for an amount of 'one-off grant' to design, build, operate and maintain the system for a predetermined concession period. The 'grant' would be funded 50% from the Section 56 Grant and 50% from the PTA, and the operator would have to allow for network expansion. The successful consortium for phase 1 (Bury–Manchester–Altrincham) would quite possibly be given the sole option for tendering for phase 1a (branches from the Altrincham line to Salford Quays and Trafford Park). If its bid were in line with its phase-1 contract, this was likely to be accepted without competition.

Tendering had been in two stages to avoid putting high costs on industry. Invitations in April 1988 produced 12 consortia responses by July as serious contenders. For the second stage, GM wanted 6 contenders but DTp insisted on 8; after choosing the eight, three of them withdrew leaving only five. Two of these were not invited to enter the second stage. There was a problem of what to include in the stage-1 tender documentation, and they were split into contractual and non-contractual areas. GM used a Reference Specification for civil work and operation, with alternatives of fixed or fluctuating prices. Three matrices, with point-scoring from 1–5 in each category were used for evaluation, one each for financial, operational and technical matters; these were combined with contractual matters into a single matrix. The tenderers were required to break down the design-and-build contract into six blocks to help tender evaluation. The final decision was expected by October 1989.

As a matter of interest, the speaker commented that the GM Economist thought that the Section 56 Grant changes might be advantageous to Metrolink phase 1. For phase 1a, private developers in Trafford and Salford Quays might be willing to put in money. Dumplington Shopping Centre still awaited approval, while the situation in Oldham and Rochdale had to be explored with DTp, and it seemed possible that a situation could arise in which the Oldham/Rochdale lines could be 'carried' by Dumplington.

PAPER 3: BIRMINGHAM'S REACTION TO THE MIDLAND METRO PROPOSALS
by Alan Wenban-Smith, Assistant Director of Development (Planning), Birmingham.

This was essentially a presentation which gave more emphasis to social rather than transport strategy in Birmingham, and dealt mainly with economic activity, local sensitivity, political leadership, and aspects where the LRT itself seemed secondary. One point he made, which seemed to be in agreement with the views of most delegates, was that the Department of Transport seemed to have over-estimated the possibility of attracting funds from developers. He emphasised that few provincial development sites had an outlook similar to that found on the Isle of Dogs, and this was reiterated in the Open Forum session; the general feeling was that developers would tend to be parochial, being happy to fund stations adjacent to their property, but little more.

PAPER 4: IMPLEMENTING URBAN RAIL: FRENCH AND WEST GERMAN SOLUTIONS
by Barry Simpson of Aston University's Transport Unit.

Mr Simpson's choice of West German cities was remarkably atypical (our comment on each is in parentheses!): München (where local policy was to replace trams by U-Bahn, until a recent apparent change in favour of trams again, and certainly hardly any LRT); Frankfurt (with four so-called U-Bahn line-groups, two of which were worked by real LRVs, one by unintended prototypes of North American LRVs, and one as 'real' Metro, and all in a metastable political situation); the third was tramless Hamburg. Just what can be deduced from this "sample" is anyone's guess. And his view of French light rail differed from ours, possibly because it seemed not to be up-to-date and not always related to LRT. But at least we could agree with him on the influence and power of French mayors, not least in connection with LRT.

PAPER 5: FURTHER IMPLEMENTATION OF LIGHT RAIL IN LONDON
by Jon Willis, Rail Development Manager of London Regional Transport.

This last paper was, like the first, of special interest to our readers at home and abroad. The financial aspects of his paper were very different from those concerning Section 56 Grants and cautioned us that saving money was not always the right approach, and did not always get the best results. His main theme was a summary of the lessons learned from Docklands and what was being done on the Beckton extension to avoid some of the problems. This was surprisingly wide-ranging and began with an indictment of light rail for being so flexible that it created its own special problems!

The problem in Docklands was that some of the more flexible features had been used to save money with no thought of what they might do to the future system. The arbitrary maximum cash limit for the initial DLR railway construction made its designers use every cost-cutting facility that light rail could offer, including running on rights-of-way disused for 2–60 years, and not always following the optimum routes. Linking them by 6% gradients and 40-metre radius curves had allowed LRT lines to run where no heavy railway could ever go, but would later constrain future operation. But it was a "this or nothing" initial situation in an environment that no-one had expected to develop into the Canary Wharf financial centre.

With hindsight, now that longer and more frequent trains would soon be running, some of the more serious problems had been identified: the tight-radius curve at Hartfield Road, north of Bow, was very noisy; the 5% gradient (the so-called "ski-jump") from the very tight triangular junction could cause slip; and this junction was so close to West India Quay station that conflicting movements were barred whenever a northbound car approached the station. And then there was that awkward 'S' bend just east of South Quay station, put in to avoid a building that was demolished before the line opened (!), and which now limited speed and even the future operation of three-car trains through that section.

Some of the DLR problems might have been hard to foresee; the resonant frequency of the steel beams straddling the concrete support beams near Cable Street was in perfect tune with the low frequencies generated by the rail-wheel contact. The DLR noise consultant likened it to a Stradivarius, but local residents were less musical. Then the station designs, following "Meccano" principles, used simple flights of steps, and there was now fear that people might slip down the straight stairs in ice and snow. Facilities for the disabled had been a great success, but designers forgot to put a window in the lifts to make them acceptable to people suffering from claustrophobia. The integration of stations into the local environment could not be afforded, and no firm development plans existed; only now could attention be paid to adequate paving, lighting and landscaping.

The Beckton extension had the same body, the London Docklands Development Corporation (LDDC), as both funder and planning authority; moreover plans for redevelopment of the Royal Docks were well advanced, and there were established residential areas which needed the new service. Here the railway planning has had to be integrated with road and development plans; this has resulted in a distinction between 'railway works' and works not essential for operation but essential for the success of the proposal.

Since a significant part of the Beckton extension would be paralleled by BR's North London Line, tracks would segregate the established residential area to the north from the development areas to the south. The LDDC had thought it important to minimise this by frequent pedestrian crossings, and with stations at the busier ones where lifts/escalators would become part of the public right-of-way. Stairs would be covered and escalators installed by arrangement with developers where passenger demand was insufficient to justify London Regional Transport or LDDC meeting the expense.

It had been decided to use a more conventional tendering process for Beckton, as distinct from the 'design and construct' feature of the contracts for the initial railway. This had been virtually imposed on the line by the need to incorporate part of the alignment and two station sites into road development work before the Bill for the extension had completed the Parliamentary process. When one considered the level of redevelopment that was taking place currently in various UK cities and the long duration of the Parliamentary and tendering stages, this illustrated a point that developers of LRT systems would have to take into account.

The Parliamentary process had taken 2½ years for Beckton and had cost dearly; it had added £4 million to the bill just because of the diversion through Canning Town, and £2.5 million because of the unexpectedly low noise limits imposed (for which the furore over the Channel Tunnel rail link must be blamed). The Lords Committee took advantage of light rail flexibility by imposing a sharply-curved alignment at Canning Town that only light rail would permit; London Regional Transport was obliged to admit to the Lords Committee that the sharp curves needed were feasible, even if not really desirable.

Mr Willis emphasised how important it was to prepare Bills adequately and not just to rush to catch the annual November deadline; while a prompt deposit added credibility, there was a great risk of the Bill failing at an early hurdle. In the discussion, a speaker illustrated this truth by citing the failure of the Heathrow Railway Bill a few days before the conference. The Bill for the Lewisham extension had been deferred for a year by London Regional Transport and would be deposited in 1989 subject to advance agreement on issues of concern to local authorities. It was unclear whether the hazardous Parliamentary Bill procedures, which local-interest groups were finding less intimidating, so that they were ready to appear without Counsel, and which were tying up increasing Parliamentary time on LRT, would be better or worse than making light rail proposals subject to the Public Enquiry process. "Railroading" an LRT Bill through Parliament was now impossible.

Finally, the Croydon proposals had not been given a full cost-benefit and engineering evaluation because consultants engaged by DTp on the South London Assessment Study had suggested that it could form the core of a more extensive LRT system. The next stage would be a Croydon Light Rail Impact Study, which would examine the impact of the scheme on the economy of the whole area, including its effects on existing office and retail businesses, redevelopment opportunities, traffic congestion, the environment and pedestrianisation. Only if this produced a positive balance would the engineering and evaluation studies be undertaken. The Croydon study would then be a prototype, providing London Regional Transport with lessons for other suburban centres.

CONCLUSIONS

In his advance conference publicity, Barry Simpson had painted a remarkably grim picture of light rail development in the UK, stating that "the pace of progress on light rail that we have seen over the last two years has slowed down". In fact, the conference showed that light rail development had progressed well past the 'hype' of scheme launches, and that positive measures were being taken to create a scenario in which LRT could be successfully implemented. At the same time, lessons were being learned from the limited UK experience with LRT, and a major point emerging was that coordination between LRT promoters and local planning bodies was needed to integrate the system into an attractive environment.

The only negative view came from an academic, rather than from anyone actually involved in light rail development, but history shows that there have always been such people. It is doubtless true that not all the schemes currently under consideration will come to fruition, but there could be no doubt that we were now in a situation of thinking more positively about introducing light rail into the major cities of the UK.

◀In Frankfurt, trams were to be removed from city streets as the U-Bahn was extended, but a metastable political situation with "Greens" holding the balance of power has led to reinstatement of surface tramways in the city centre. *G.H. Köhler*

▶▲Forty-metre radius curves on the Docklands Light Railway allowed LRT to run where no heavy rail could ever go, but this elevated junction at Poplar will need substantial reconstruction to accomodate the Beckton extension. *F.W. Schneider III*

▶In Nantes the new light rail line was built despite the opposition of the Mayor. Within a year 40 000 passengers had switched from private car to public transport. Now the Mayor has welcomed the extension of line 1 and plans for line 2. *M.R. Taplin*

Stratford
02
Docklands
G

M1 308

AVON METRO
Can Private Enterprise Succeed

by John Symons and Michael Taplin

Ten years ago, Richard Cottrell (then the MEP for Bristol) launched his campaign for a light rail transit system to serve the Bristol conurbation, which since 1974 has comprised the greater part of the county of Avon. In 1979 he was advocating the development of a metro network using principles very similar to those then being adopted by the Tyneside PTE based on Newcastle. These involved the electrification of local railway lines, and construction of a 5 km tunnel under the centre of Bristol which would have acted as the main trunk of the system. Mr Cottrell's study failed to convince the various authorities involved that the scheme would justify the not-inconsiderable outlay for the development of the network (more than £216 million).

Since then Bristol's traffic problems have continued to get worse, with increasing traffic congestion taking its toll on the largely road-based transport network. In 1986 Mr Cottrell and a small group of architect and planning colleagues formed a company, Advanced Transport for Avon Ltd (ATA), to promote a modified version of the 1979 proposals. These were worked up in sufficient detail for a parliamentary Bill for the first stage to be deposited in November 1987. The scheme is different from all the other UK schemes lodged with Parliament in that it is promoted by a private company rather than a local authority, with the promise of private funding, and as such faced formidable problems in convincing local authorities, landowners, British Rail and the financial institutions of its merits.

The scheme is also different from the 1979 proposals in that it features surface operation on the streets of Bristol rather than the expensive tunnel section under the city centre. Phase 1 (60 km) was costed at around £195 million in 1988, a significant reduction when compared with the higher cost of the 1979 scheme, and much more likely to succeed therefore.

ATA has designed a network of lines based on two criteria: the failure of the existing rail network to satisfy the needs of those travelling to central Bristol due to the poor location of Temple Meads station, and the use of redundant or under-exploited rail lines which extend into potential growth areas. In particular ATA looked at the growth areas in Northavon District and on the eastern fringe of Bristol – along the M4 motorway corridor – plus the rapidly growing residential areas on the banks of the Severn estuary at Portbury and Portishead. There are also various changes in land-use patterns in the rather spread-out inner city of Bristol (now including an area administered by the Urban Development Corporation) which require proper public transport links, and an overloaded road network between Bristol and its neighbouring city Bath.

The network which evolved is based on existing rail trackage, reinstatement of former lines and construction of new tracks, principally in central Bristol, south Bristol and to serve new developments at Cribbs Causeway, Bradley Stoke and Yate in north Avon. The complete scheme comprises two phases:

Phase 1

(i) the existing tracks of the railway from Portishead to Ashton Gate, with a new spur to the docks branch leading to an off-centre terminal at Wapping Wharf (Bill 1);
(ii) new street tracks from Wapping Wharf across Prince St bridge and through the commercial and shopping centre of Bristol to Tower Bridge, Victoria St and a new station adjacent to Temple Meads BR (Bill 2);
(iii) alongside BR tracks from Temple Meads via Lawrence Hill and Stapleton Rd to Filton, then new street reservation on branches to Bradley Stoke and Cribbs Causeway (Bill 3);
(iv) from Lawrence Hill along the former railway line through Fishponds, Kingswood, Mangotsfield and Emersons Green to Yate (Bill 3);
(v) a new branch from Temple Meads via the UDC area to St Philip's Marsh and St Anne's (Bill 3);

Phase 2

(vi) incorporation of the existing BR branch to Severn Beach with a new direct link from Clifton Down to the city centre at Haymarket;
(vii) a south Bristol loop linking Wapping Wharf with Bedminster, Hartcliffe, Knowle and St Philip's Marsh;
(vii) extensions from Yate to Thornbury, Portishead to Clevedon and Cribbs Causeway to Severn Beach;
(viii) a complementary service over BR tracks from Weston-Super-Mare to Bath. (BR trains in ATA livery?).

These routes would be operated by modern light rail vehicles featuring low-floor access and overhead current collection. Sixty cars would be needed eventually. Driver operation is proposed with articulated cars 28 m long and 2.6 m wide, capable of taking 25 m curves and carrying up to 200 passengers. Branches are expected to offer a 10-minute service between 06.00 and 24.00 seven days/week (with a later start on Sundays).

Avon Light Rail Transit Bill No. 1 was deposited on 27 November 1987 to provide powers to build and operate the 17 km line from Wapping Wharf to Portishead. The Bill included provision for ATA to take over sections of the Portishead Railway and Wapping line currently owned by British Rail, but without any passenger service. New works include the Ashton Gate connecting curve and nearby depot. There is provision for an interchange between road and rail traffic at Easton-in-Gordano (adjacent to the M5 motorway), where an important 600-plus vehicle park-and-ride facility is intended. There will be 10 stops, five on the site of previous railway stations, though no specific consent is required to open additional stations on any site within railway land.

Avon County Council and Bristol City Council lodged petitions against the Bill, both in principle and detail. Both supported the general concept of light rail transit for Avon, and the County Council objection was withdrawn after detail discussion with and the receipt of assurances on various aspects

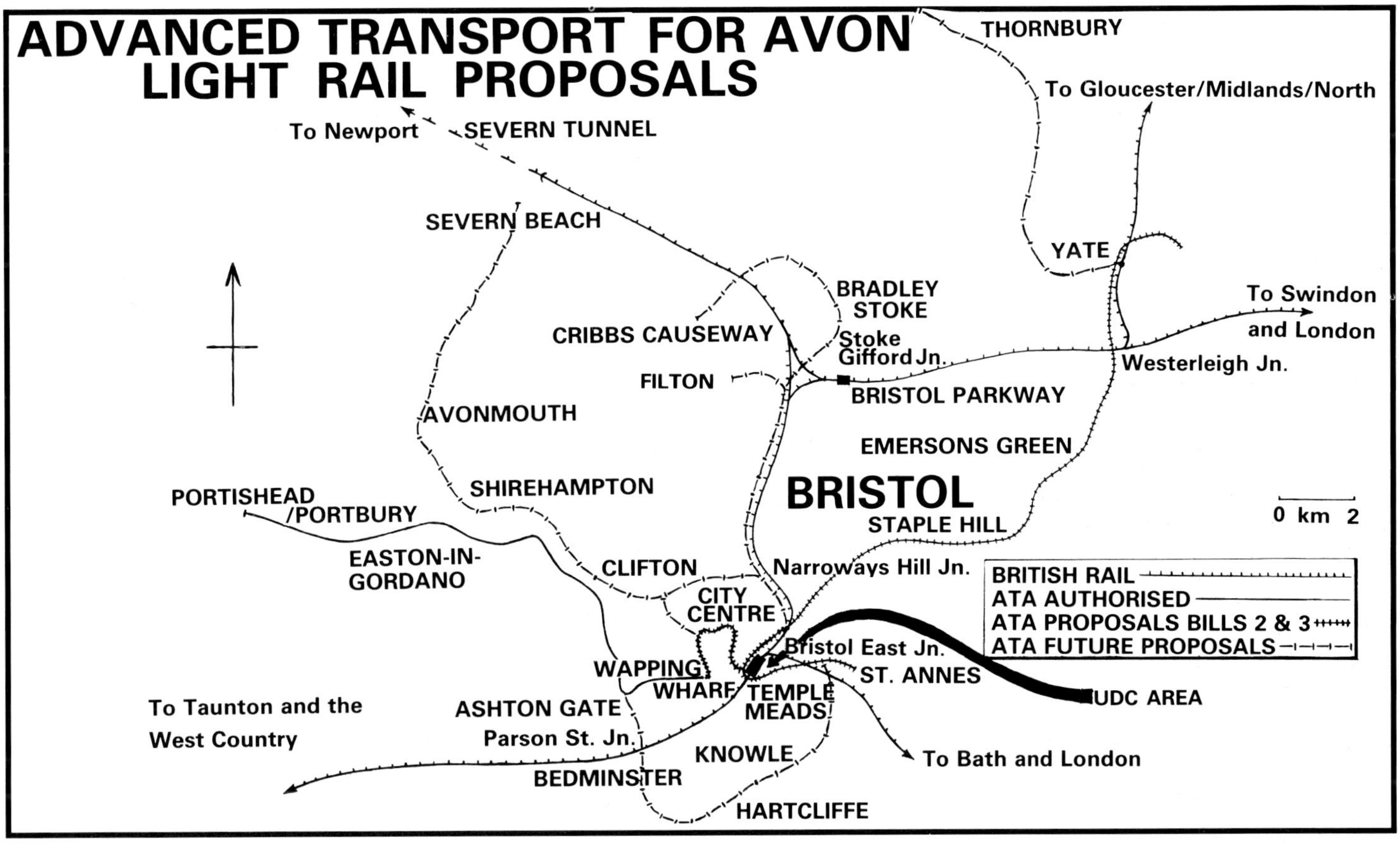

from the promoters. The opposition of Bristol City Council took rather longer to overcome, but was largely quashed in September 1988 when the city agreed to grant ATA licence to run over council land. A similar agreement was reached later with British Rail. An undertaking was given to the Port of Bristol that the line would be built to sufficient standard to permit freight trains to run over it should a freight connection to the Royal Portbury Dock be required in the future. Parliamentary progress was delayed for some time by one of Bristol's MPs, but the Bill secured its second reading in January 1989 and Royal Assent was received on 11th May 1989, a significant milestone in ATA's progress. The parliamentary delay to the first Bill caused submission of a second Bill, for the street-running section in the city centre, to be deferred from November 1988.

In the meantime, given that any proposal for street running needs the consent of Avon County Council as highway authority (under Standing Order 25 of both Houses of Parliament), the County Council and ATA have been jointly working on the detail of Bill 2 to ensure that all aspects are fully considered and that a proper process of consultation is carried out.

Much of the opposition to the Bill in principle stemmed from concern over whether ATA had the financial resources necessary to construct and operate the system. At first the company indicated that all the necessary finance would be raised privately from the following sources: equity and limited recourse debt against future revenue, together with advertising, sale of franchises and right-of-way rentals, plus contributions from developers who stood to gain from enhanced land values in the vicinity of the line when it was completed. However ATA has since made it clear that it will be applying to the government for grant under section 56 of the Transport Act 1968, and given the Government support for the Bill at the Second Reading stage in the House of Commons, presumably feels confident that such grant will be forthcoming. The system is predicted to more than cover its operating cost from revenue.

In early 1989 it was announced that two development companies had made a substantial but undisclosed investment in the project; Parkdale PLC and the Dutch-based VOM International became major shareholders in a new company, Avon Developments Ltd, with ATA as a minority shareholder. The new company is examining a selected number of development and investment opportunities along the ATA routes. The Chairman of ADL is a director of VOM and involved with the Emersons Green development that will be served by an ATA route. ATA has indicated that it will not run the system itself, but will licence the operation to a company on a contract basis, and it is known that more than one bus company has expressed an interest in obtaining this licence.

Following the granting of the Act of Parliament, ATA announced that it had secured the £3.5 million necessary to take it through to the start of construction of line 1 in summer 1990. In the meantime Bills 2 and 3 will be submitted to Parliament in November 1989. It is hoped to open the Portishead line to passenger traffic in 1992, and the continuation through the city centre to Temple Meads in 1993. The Portishead line is predicted to carry 250 000 passengers annually. No date has yet been given for completion of the 60 km £80 million Portishead–Yate/Cribbs Causeway line.

ATA are a small private company, and when their proposals were announced there were many who predicted that no more progress would be made than in 1979. However they have shown that is is possible for private promoters to win parliamentary approval for a new railway (after all, they point out, most of Britain's railways were built this way in another era) and the directors are understandably bullish about their ability to see the project through to completion. Of course there are still the doubters, and those with a political axe to grind over what they see as the detrimental effects of property speculation on the community. When the project succeeds it will be further evidence of the ability of private capital to fund public transport projects.

Late news is that the project evaluation for Bills 2 and 3, required in particular to satisfy Avon County Council, is behind schedule, which may delay Parliamentary progress in the 1989/90 session.

LIGHT RAIL TRANSIT

Current Developments in Great Britain

by Michael Taplin, Chairman LRTA

When the Light Railway Transport League (now LRTA) was founded in 1937, to campaign for the retention and modernisation of Britain's tramways, everyone understood the terms tramway and tramcar (the latter often shortened to tram) and the magazine title The Modern Tramway represented all we stood for. However the first two words of the League's title were remarkably prophetic, as if our founders realised that the humble tram might become stuck with hackneyed and unwelcome adjectives such as clanking and grinding, and require a new image. With the British urban transport trends of the 1940s and 1950s almost wholly against the League's objectives, this was probably a wise move.

In continental Europe only France turned against *le tramway* in such a wholehearted way (as in Britain, for reasons based more on national attitudes to public transport rather than sound transport planning), but in America the term streetcar acquired a similar pejorative connatation. In that era we tended to look to the United States if we wanted to see where Britain would be in 10 years time, and planners started talking about transportation and transit to show how forward thinking they were. What most British people called the underground (since London was the only system of significant size) was heavy rapid transit in American planning terminology (subway in the vernacular).

The LRTL often referred to modern light railways when describing continental developments, since in those days of little mass travel overseas, the use of foreign words to convey concepts would not have meant much. In the 1960s the use of light rapid transit came into vogue, to differentiate from heavy rapid transit, but this phrase was soon in danger of being hijacked to embrace the so-called innovative transit systems that were all the rage for a period, mainly automated guideways with small cars.

In 1972 the US Department of Transportation published a report entitled Light Rail Transit Systems – a Definition and Evaluation. This was unequivocal: Light Rail Transit uses vehicles with steel wheels that operate on steel rails. At the same time the Boeing company was trying to break in to the urban transit market, and when it won the contract to provide new cars to the Boston and San Francisco tramways, it launched the US Standard Light Rail Vehicle with all the hype that might be expected of an aerospace manufacturer. Light rail transit had arrived.

The LRTL now found itself in august company with Federal reports advocating all that it stood for, and US industry busy jumping on the bandwaggon. The fact that it tried to reinvent the wheel, and failed, is part of another story, but fortunately there was the experience and expertise from continental Europe to carry through the success story. The semantics took root, and soon British transport planners were beginning to take notice of light rail. The expanded magazine title of Modern Tramway and Light Railway Review, introduced with the launch on the bookstalls in January 1962, went through a rapid metamorphosis of subtitle to Rapid Transit Review in 1974, and Light Rapid Transit in 1977, to Light Rail Transit from 1 January 1980, when the Light Railway Transport League became the Light Rail Transit Association.

Domestic considerations disposed of, there was still a problem of terminology for light rapid transit tended to be used interchangeably with light rail transit, including by some of the promoters of the schemes described below (particularly Manchester, though even they have now started to also use the term Supertram coined by South Yorkshire). We have been rescued by the United Kingdom Department of Transport 1989 guidance notes covering the highway and vehicle engineering aspects of street-running systems. Here light rapid transit is defined as any guided transit system used for the carriage of passengers where the characteristics of the vehicles do not conform to those required for main line railways.

This may seem rather quaint to our foreign readers, particularly those in Europe whose statutes are based on Roman law, where the difference between main line and other railways is not so crucial in regard to fencing requirements as with British statute, derived from the English common law and the duty of the state to protect its citizens. However it clarifies that light rail transit systems are within the definition of light rapid transit, but not all light rapid transit systems are light rail transit.

Thus light rapid transit includes automated guideway systems running on rubber tyres, and monorails as well as the conventional steel wheel light rail systems that feature in most British proposals. The Docklands Light Railway is clearly properly so named, even though it features automatic train control, while the Newcastle Metro is light rail transit, though it too is fully segregated and signalled. Introduction of the word metro prompts a reminder that there is now no clear division between light rail transit and metro (short for metropolitan railway as well as the French derivation, and increasingly used as a snappy alternative to heavy rapid transit), but rather a gradual gradation from one to the other with much depending on local conditions. Indeed the French tend to call light rail transit pre-metro. This backs up the definition supported by the Light Rail Commission of the International Union of Public Transport (UITP), which forms the basis for our own description below.

LIGHT RAIL TRANSIT (LRT)

LRT is a term used to describe a rail-based urban passenger transit system of intermediate capacity (between bus and the full metropolitan railway) used to meet public demand qualitatively and quantatively at an acceptable cost. The system is normally electrically powered and generally segregated from other traffic, but often with flexibility for mixed running where segregation cannot be achieved at reasonable cost. In its simplest form it can be regarded as a modern tramway, but it is capable of being developed in stages to a fully-segregated system: each development stage can be the final stage, but allows for subsequent development to further stages, permitting improvements to be utilised without delay.

Various degrees of technical innovation can be incorporated up to fully-automatic driverless operation, though the latter does imply total segregation (elevated, sub-surface or fully-fenced surface) at considerable cost. The system can use existing railway right-of-way and in certain circumstances mix with other rail traffic.

In comparison with a metropolitan railway LRT is normally used to provide more frequent and shorter-distance services, and is less expensive to build and operate. Compared to buses LRT can cost-effectively provide capacity for passenger flows peaking in excess of 2000 passengers/hr, and provide a more reliable high-quality service that attracts non-bus users to public transport.

There are over 300 systems with LRT features worldwide and in recent years LRT has been increasingly used for new urban transport projects, particularly in North America, where 10 new systems have been built in the last nine years. Now there is increasing interest in Great Britain, with three systems falling within the light rail category in operation, three more authorised and several others at various stages of planning. These are described below.

▲Ten new light rail systems have been built in North America in the last nine years and more are planned. Portland, Oregon, has one of the best examples combining street track in a rejuvenated city centre with street reservations and use of abandoned railway alignment in the suburbs. *S.J. Morgan*

►Automated mini-metros have to be totally segregated, with at-grade portions securely fenced for safety reasons. This is the French VAL system in Lille. *M. Vieugels*

◄The Blackpool tramway operates largely on reservation along the holiday resort's seafront, then on private right-of-way to the neighbouring market town of Fleetwood, which features classic street track. New and modernised cars have arrived in recent years. *M.R. Taplin*

▼The Tyne and Wear Metro marked the start of the urban rail revival in Great Britain and introduced many light rail features for the first time. *G.B. Clayton*

BLACKPOOL

The sole survivor of British tramways runs over 18 km of largely segregated track carrying about 6 million passengers/annum, providing a regular service throughout the year and a summer tourist attraction. After a period of little change, new cars have been purchased and a programme of track improvements carried out, with some financial assistance from Lancashire County Council.

TYNE & WEAR

Planned in the early 1970s as the essential part of an integrated passenger transport system for Newcastle and surrounding towns, the Tyne & Wear metro was designed to use existing BR tracks, with new tunnels to reach the city centre. Opened in 1980, it has grown to 56 route km with

▼The Docklands Light Railway is playing a vital role in the regeneration of London Docklands by providing attractive and accessible transport links. *F.W. Schneider III*

44 stations carrying 47 million passengers annually. A further low cost 3.5 km extension to Newcastle Airport has been authorised and should be built by 1991. Studies continue on other possible extensions, including Washington and Sunderland. With its fully segregated and signalled tracks the Metro is at the heavy end of the light rail spectrum.

LONDON

Docklands Light Railway. The initial 12 km system opened for public service in August 1987 and was promoted by the London Docklands Development Corporation with central government finance. Initially designed to carry 2000 passengers/hr, the 1.8 km city extension to Bank now under construction (with private finance) and the massive office developments on the Isle of Dogs will require more cars and higher frequencies to carry up to 20 000 passengers/hr. About 10.5 million passengers were carried in 1988. Summer 1989 saw the authorisation of a 7.5 km surface extension to Beckton, and consultation is in progress on a cross-river link to Greenwich and Lewisham. New orders will take the present fleet of 11 cars to 65 by 1992. The use of new elevated structures and old railway alignments has made possible a fully-segregated system with "driverless" trains.

Other London schemes. In 1986 London Regional Transport and Network South-East (BR) published the report of a joint study of the possible scope for light rail elsewhere in London, identifying some 30 opportunities. As a result a major scheme for the Croydon area was chosen for detailed study by consultants. It involves the conversion and extension of BR lines with new low-cost stations, plus a street running link across the centre of Croydon. The report was published in 1988 and recommends that three of the lines studied and the central link should proceed. Consultation with the Borough Council is in progress.

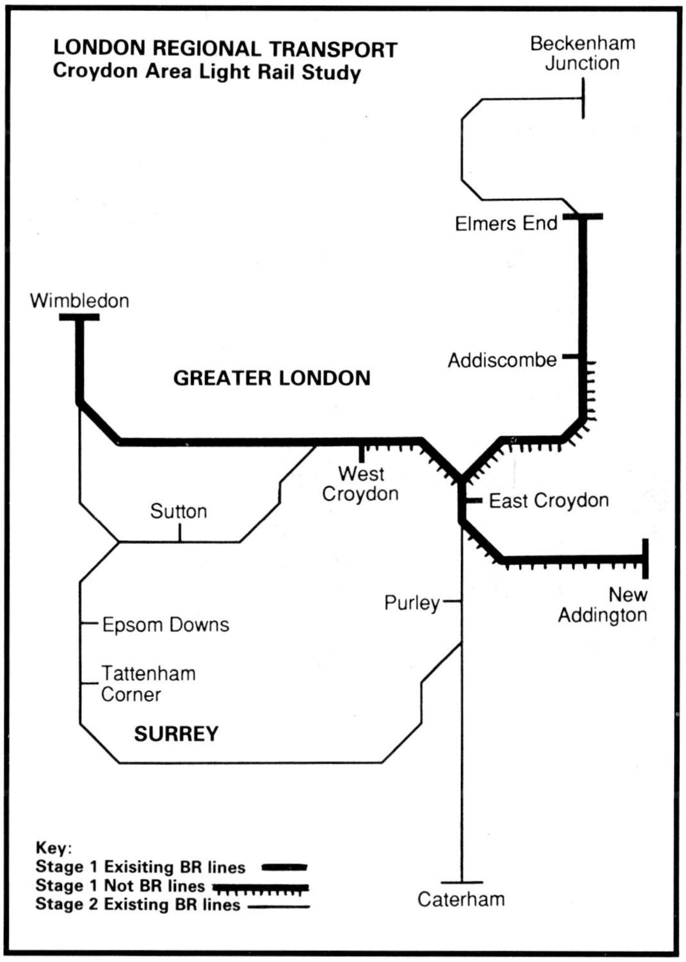

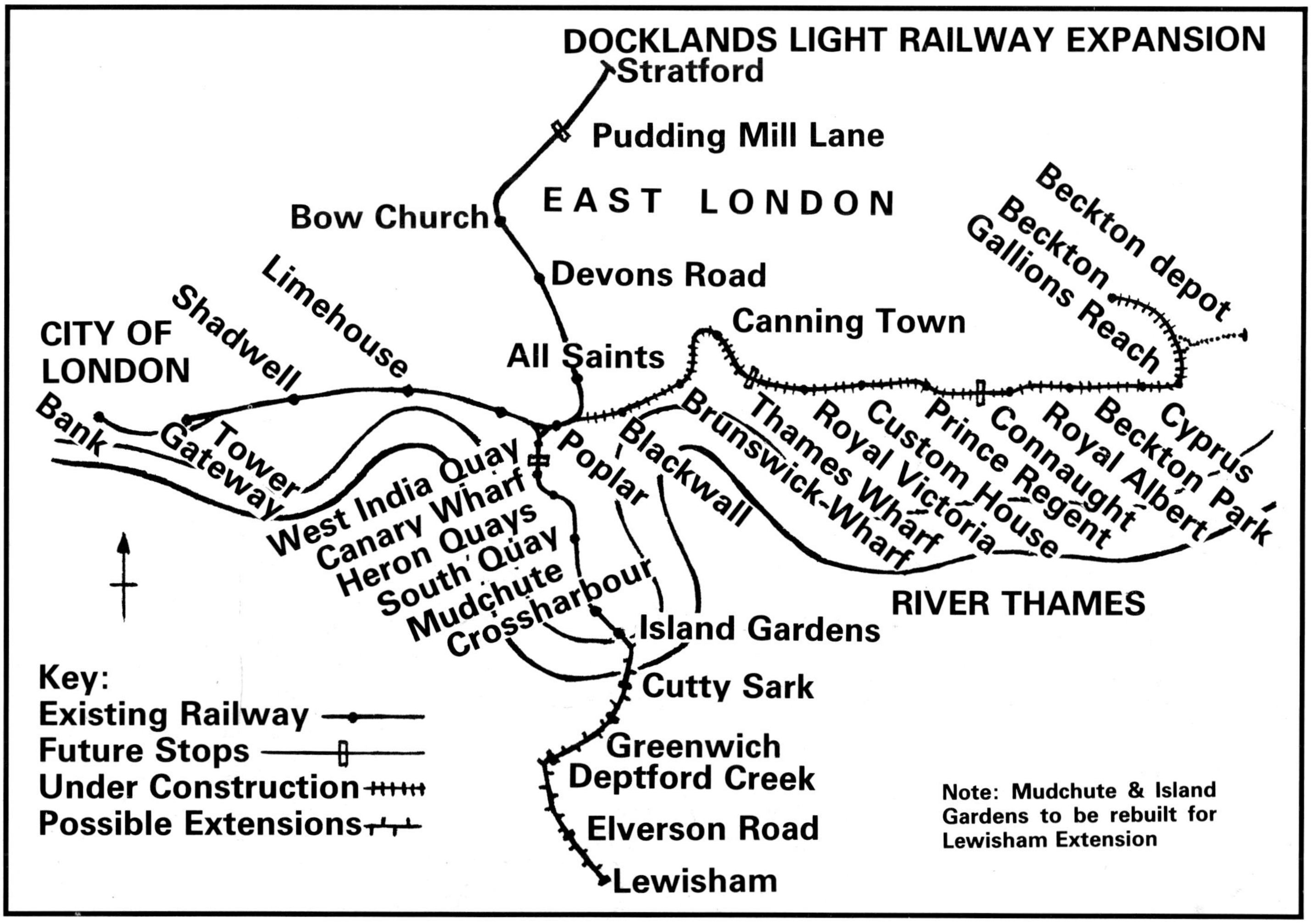

MANCHESTER

Greater Manchester PTE are promoting a scheme for the construction in stages of a 100 km network of light rail lines based on existing BR tracks, but with 3 km of street running to link the existing peripheral railway stations with the city centre. The enabling Bills for the 32 km first phase linking Bury and Altrincham have been passed by Parliament and a government grant approved (subject to the involvement of the private sector in the financing package). Contracts for the construction and operation of the first line were to be let in autumn 1989 and the Metrolink should open in 1991. Further extensions to serve the Salford Quays dockland redevelopment and the Trafford Park industrial estate are proposed with a Bill seeking authorisation put before Parliament in November 1988.

SOUTH YORKSHIRE

The South Yorkshire PTE deposited a Parliamentary Bill in November 1985 for a 22 km light rail line across Sheffield. The line is based on highway alignments but with about 50% segregation through the use of reserved tracks. The Bill completed its passage through Parliament in October 1988. A second Bill was deposited in November 1988 for a line to the Lower Don Valley, a major regeneration area and site for the World Student Games in 1991. In June 1989 the government indicated approval in principle, subject to further cost/benefit analysis and involvement of the private sector. Tenders have been invited for design and construction, with separate tenders for operation and maintenance to follow.

AVON

A private company Advanced Transport for Avon has produced plans for a regional light rail network based on Bristol and deposited a Parliamentary Bill for the first line (17 km wholly on existing or disused BR alignments) in November 1987; this received Royal Assent in May 1989. After delay caused by political controversy in Bristol, Bills for the second stage, 43 km including street running through the city centre should be deposited in November 1989. ATA is associated with property development companies.

WEST MIDLANDS

In September 1987 the West Midlands PTE launched its Midland Metro project for regional system covering Birmingham and the Black Country. Extensive consultation is in progress with all interested parties, including private developers and the European Regional Development Fund for financing. A bill for the first line (19 km, Birmingham–Wolverhampton) was deposited in November 1988, involving mostly disused BR alignments, but with some street running at Wolverhampton. Further corridors in Birmingham and between Wolverhampton and Walsall have been identified for a 1989 Bill.

WEST YORKSHIRE

The West Yorkshire PTE's development strategy for public transport includes the reintroduction of trolleybuses in Bradford and a 21 km street based (but 90% reserved track) light rail system for Leeds. Consultants worked up details so that a Bill for the first line could be deposited in Parliament in November 1988, but political controversy within Leeds City Council caused this to be withdrawn, and further consultation is in progress on the form the scheme should take.

SOUTHAMPTON

In November 1988 Southampton City Council lodged a Parliamentary Bill for an elevated people-mover line around the city centre, hoping that the line can be financed by contributions from commercial interests involved in city centre retailing and development.

SOUTH HAMPSHIRE

In 1988 Hampshire County Council engaged consultants to carry out a study of light rail potential in the Gosport and Portsmouth areas. They identified the feasibility of a line in the Fareham–Gosport–Portsmouth corridor, and this is now the subject of local consultation.

SCOTLAND

Both Lothian Regional Council (Edinburgh) and Strathclyde PTE (Glasgow) are undertaking studies into the possible role for light rail. The initial results of the Edinburgh study recommended a six route light rail option for construction by 1996, and these proposals are now subject to consultation.

TEESSIDE

The Teesside Development Corporation and Cleveland County Council have jointly funded a study into the potential for light rail in Cleveland.Consultants have identified a core route linking Stockton and Middlesbrough offering significant benefits and the scheme is now being worked up in detail.

LIVERPOOL

The Merseyside Development Corporation is investigating the potential for light rail over the route of the former Overhead Railway, while the PTE is looking at routes to the eastern suburbs.

NOTTINGHAM

Nottingham Development Enterprise, backed by city and county councils, has suggested a light rail system for greater Nottingham and a feasibility study into a Nottingham–Hucknall line took place in 1989 with positive results.

SWINDON

In 1989 Wiltshire County Council commissioned consultants for a transportation study that includes examination of the potential for light rail in the Swindon area.

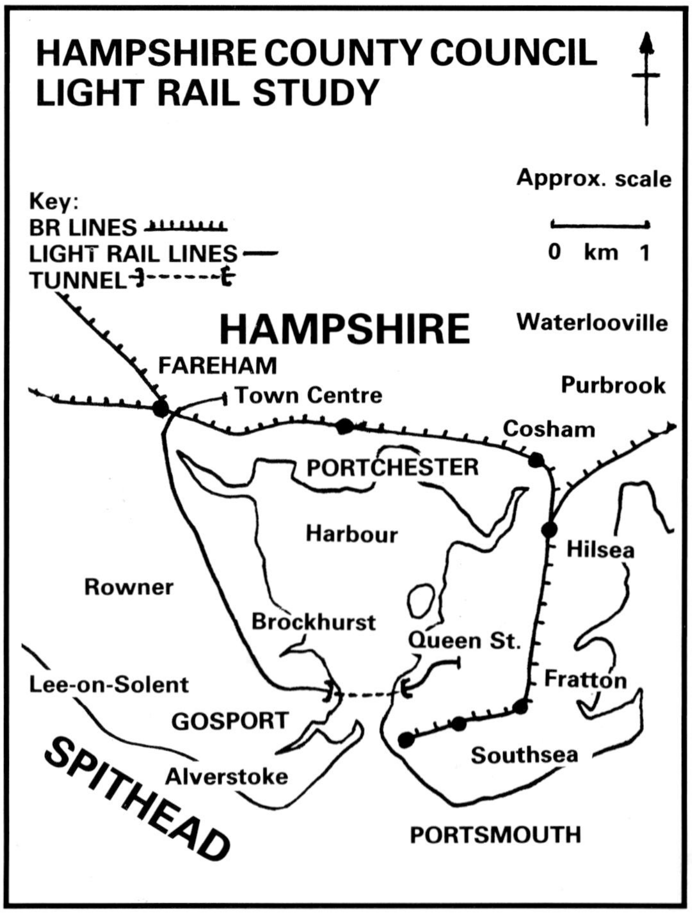

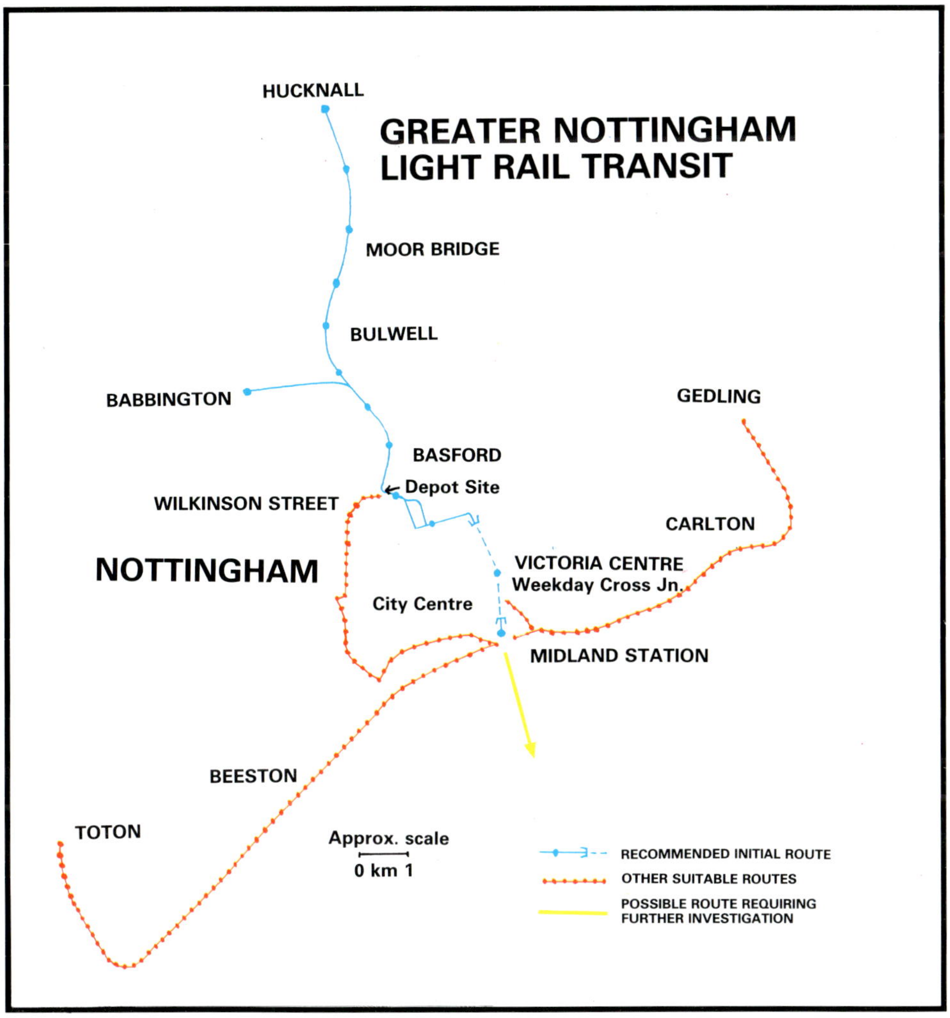

CARDIFF

Consultants retained by the Cardiff Bay Development Corporation are proposing a light rail link from the Central Station to Cardiff Docks via the new South Glamorgan County Council offices.

GLOUCESTER

The City tourist plan includes a street-based tramway link between the city centre and the redevelopment site at the historic Gloucester docks. Detailed consultation is in progress with developers who may provide financing opportunities. This will be an example of the heritage tramway concept that is proving successful in the USA (either free-standing or in association with a light rail scheme).

OTHERS

In addition to the above published proposals, several other locations have light rail under consideration, including Cambridge, Chester, Hull, Norwich, Reading, and Plymouth. Studies in Aberdeen do not appear to indicate that a light rail scheme is feasible.

▼The Docklands Light Railway attracted much media attention, which raised lay perceptions of light rail considerably.
M.R. Taplin

References: Modern Tramway 1987–9; Local Transport Today, 1989;
Light Rail '87 (LRTA 1987); Provisional LRT Guidance Note (DTp, 1989);
Light Rail Trends (UITP, 1989); Light Rail Transit (PTE Group, 1988);
Light Rail for London (London Transport, September 1986);
Light Rail: some implications for the South-East, SERPLAN, 1988

Light rail can be an important catalyst in urban regeneration. The top photograph is a 1984 view of a rundown part of the city centre in Portland, USA.

In 1986 light rail came to Portland and the bottom photograph shows how it has attracted life back into a revitalised city centre.

S.J. Morgan

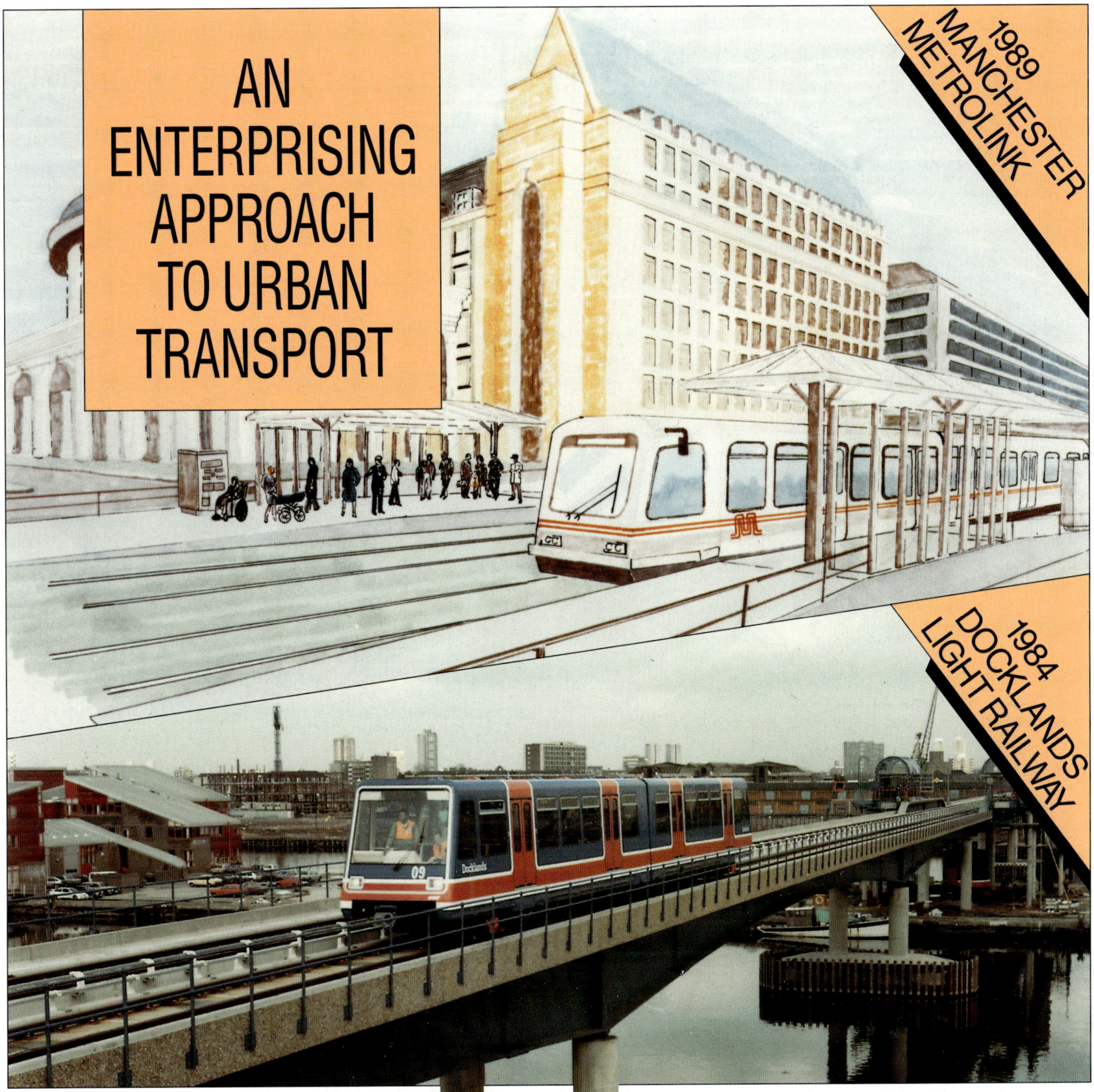

In less than three years the GEC Mowlem Railway Group designed and built the remarkable hi-tech rail transit system for London Docklands, on time and within budget – a really successful turnkey project. Now the GMA Group, in which Mowlem is a major partner, has been invited to design, build and, this time operate the new Manchester Metrolink.

Two major urban transport projects, bringing new life to inner city environments. Mowlem has the vision, expertise and experience to help you to be a driving force for progress in your area.

Mowlem

Mowlem Civil Engineering,
Foundation House, Eastern Road, Bracknell, Berkshire
RG12 2UZ. Tel: 0344 426826 Fax: 0344 862027

IMPROVED ACCESS FOR ALL

Low-Floor Light Rail Vehicles

by Michael Taplin, Chairman, LRTA

In order to maximise patronage, and in particular to attract riders from their own cars, public transport must be comfortable and efficient. Comfort does not just mean a quiet and smooth ride in agreeable surroundings, but also ease of boarding and alighting from the vehicle. This also has a direct effect on efficiency, by minimising stop dwell times, thus maximising the commercial speed and requiring fewer vehicles and staff to provide a given level of service.

The ideal way to speed boarding and alighting from a rail transit car is station platforms level with the floor of the car; all heavy rapid transit systems have this feature, to handle large numbers of passengers (though access to the platform from the street is another matter). Some light rail systems (e.g. Utrecht, Istanbul, Manila and Calgary) are able to adopt high platforms because all their stations are on segregated sites or (in the case of Calgary) the design of the system permits platforms in the street. High platforms are rarely feasible at every stop on an upgraded tramway, and on new light rail systems may not be adopted due to a trade-off against the need to use the inherent flexibility of light rail to fit the system in to its surroundings.

The floor height of a rail transit car is a function of what has to be accomodated beneath the floor (wheel sets and running gear) and what other space is available for what is traditionally underfloor (motors, controller, transformer, batteries, compressor, air cylinders etc). The former usually dictate a minimum floor height over the bogies of 800–900 mm;

Street operation in Calgary is limited to a transit mall, so high platforms have been built on the highway to permit level access to light rail cars. *Siemens*

A new light rail system may be able to adopt high platforms throughout because all their stations are on segregated sites. This is the Utrecht–Nieuwegein line in the Netherlands. *R.N.H. Jones*

▲Since 1989 Basel's route 10 has been worked by coupled sets of articulated cars, with the lead car an example rebuilt with a new low-floor centre section. *M.R. Taplin*

◀The low-floor centre section of Basel's eight-axle cars is a boon for mothers with prams and buggies. The hooks on the left are for the other main group of passengers, cyclists. *M.R. Taplin*

over non-motored bogies a lower height may be achieved. As I wrote in "Geneva takes the plunge" (Modern Tramway, May 1985), engineers have been trying to overcome this problem for over 50 years.

The solutions they tested had a cost in both mechanical complexity and the price of the car, a cost operators were generally unwilling to meet while there were plenty of passengers able to climb four steps from the street. Now the market demands a user-friendly system, and society demands that the needs of less-mobile members of the community are given every consideration. Some research suggests that 20 per cent of the population suffers from some form of mobility impairment, and neither commercial managers nor politicians can afford to overlook this fact. Different design engineers have taken a fresh look at the problem and come up with different solutions.

The simplest approach is to lower the floor between the bogies and place the doorways in this section. Since the space over the bogies cannot be wasted, this means interior steps, but poor design can reduce the passenger flow and capacity within the car, and create a potential for tripping accidents. On an articulated car a wide and level access through the articulation is needed, particularly if wheelchairs are carried. The gradients on the system or the technical design of the car may require motors in all bogies. On older systems a proportion of passengers may have to pay their fare on the car, so a door needs to be by the driver and thus adjacent to the front bogie, with no room in the overhang for a proper low floor section, and steps to the rest of the car. On an interurban car none of this matters so much and three Swiss lines (BD, RBS, WSB) are planning the joint purchase of 22 cars to an eight-axle design with a 390 mm floor height between conventional bogies (about 50 per cent of the floor area).

On an eight-axle tram with Jacobs bogies the (normally) smaller centre section offers a structurally-simple solution by confining the low floor section and corresponding doorway(s) to this part of the car. This is the solution adopted by Amsterdam, Basel (BLT) and Freiburg, achieving floor heights in the range 280–325 mm (one step from the street or level access from a low platform). Amsterdam and Basel built prototype low-floor sections to test the concept on existing cars: Basel needed extra capacity and chose this method to lengthen its six-axle trams to eight-axle cars; Amsterdam needed new cars and was able to incorporate the results of its trials in their specification. Both feature central gangway steps to the rest of the car (floor height around 850 mm) Freiburg are modifying their existing design for new cars on order. Würzburg, with tight clearances and the requirement for all axles motored, modified their initial specification to make space for two wheelchairs with steps giving access to a side gangway ramped to the 910 mm high floors of the suspended articulation portals to the end sections. Few seats, if any, and limited space in the low-floor area of all these transitional designs give the appearance of a compromise, with mobility-impaired passengers confined to one entrance only, and boarding/alighting not speeded by much.

◄Another German design of low-floor car is that built by LHB for Würzburg. With all axles motored the low-floor is confined to the centre section. *LHB, courtesy Railway Gazette International*

►The biggest fleet of low-floor cars so far is the 54 ordered from Fiat by Torino. The short central section rests on an unmotored bogie with independent wheels. *R.N.H. Jones*

►▼On the new Grenoble system all stops have 280 mm high platforms, facilitating near-level access into the cars. *Peter Fox*

►▼▼The interior of the Grenoble car looking from the low-floor section and showing steps up to the normal floor level over the motored bogies. *M.R. Taplin*

◄The Vevey non-motored bogie for Bern, designed to permit a low-floor through the centre section of the eight-axle car. *Vevey*

▼The Geneva design for a six-axle low-floor car has been adapted by Vevey for the French system at St Etienne. Note that the central bogie does not support the articulation. *Vevey*

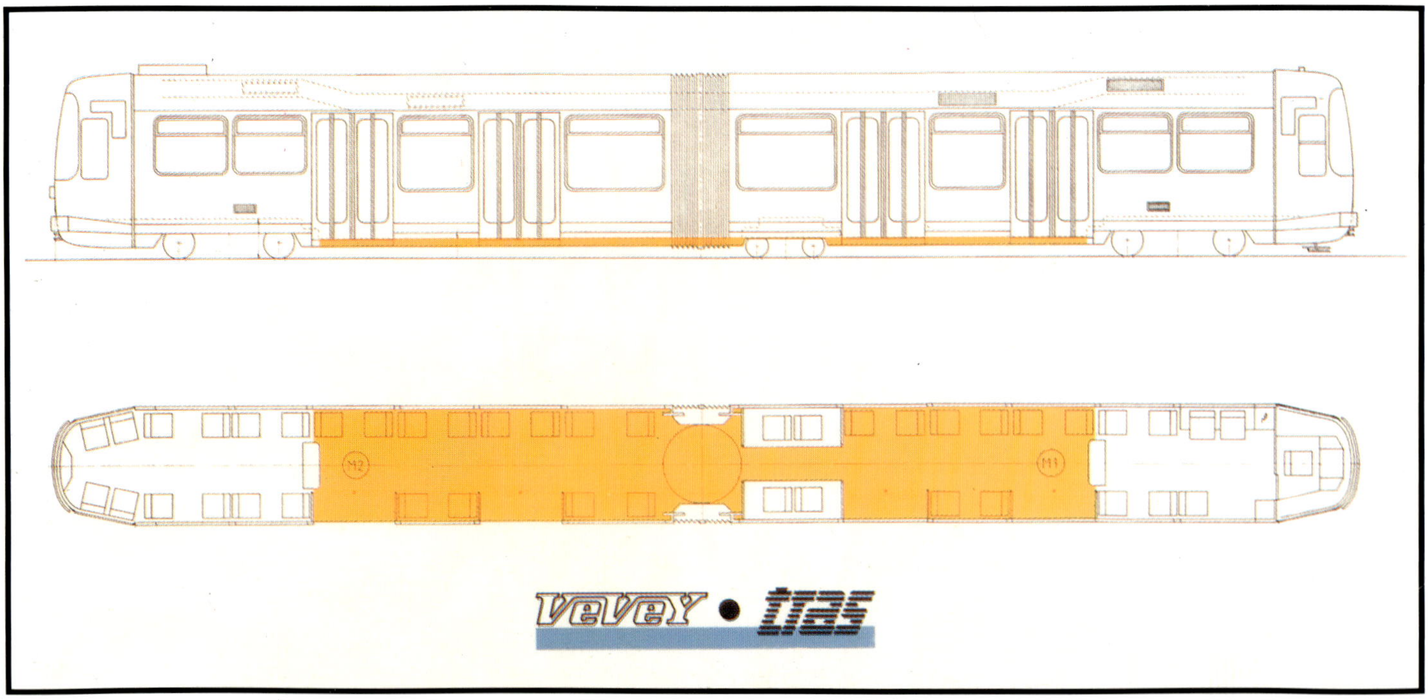

▼The prototype Vevey low-floor car for Genève shows the door location, with a step that folds down on opening to give two-step (260 + 220 mm) access from the street. *W.J. Wyse*

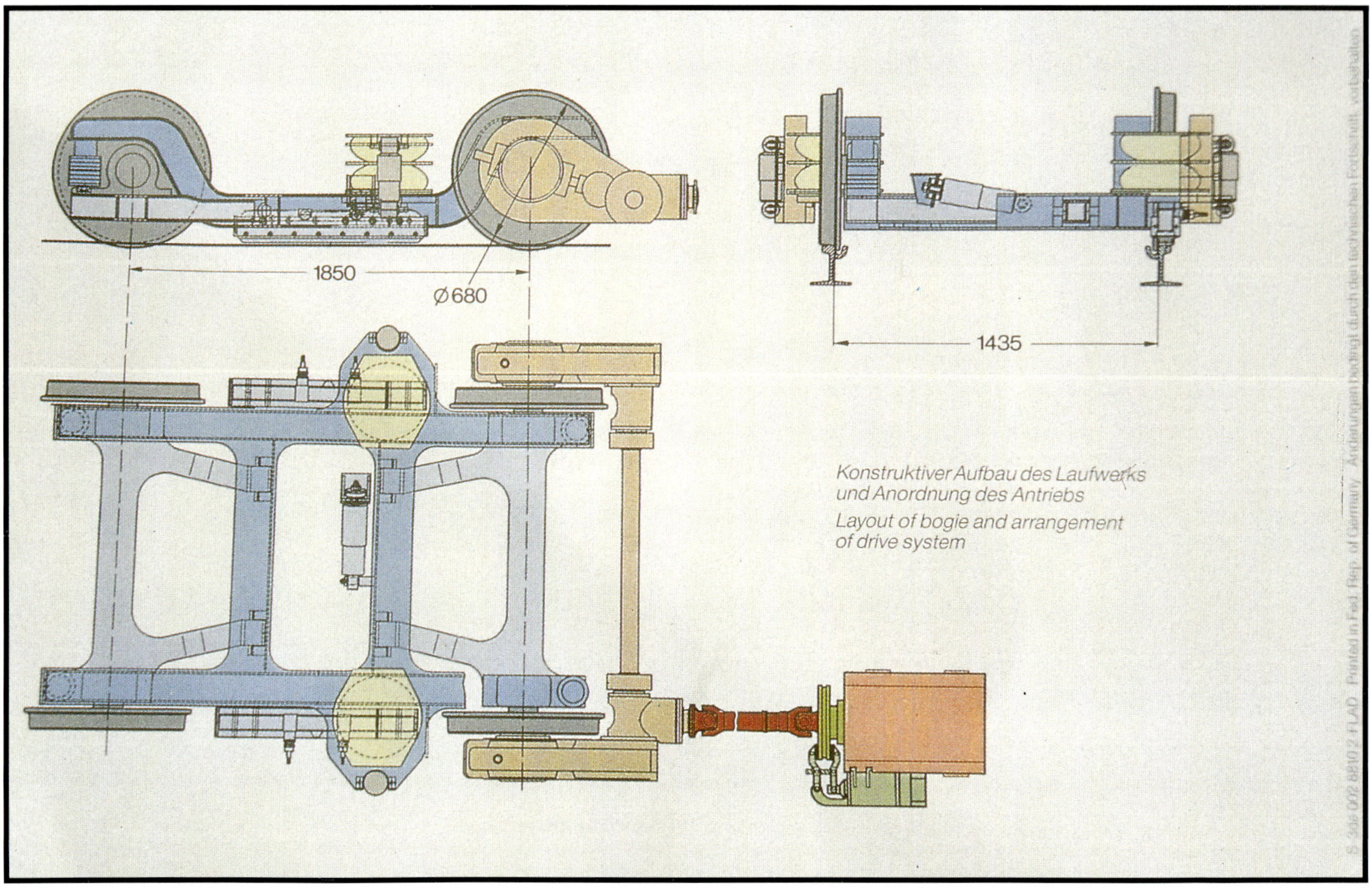

▲The bogie design developed by MAN-GHH and soon to appear under prototype cars in Bremen and München. The motor is body-mounted, driving through a cardan shaft. *MAN-GHH*

◀The radical SOCIMI prototype which commenced trials at Milano in 1989 features a 350 mm floor throughout the car thanks to its novel bogie design. *SOCIMI*

◀▼The SOCIMI bogie with four motors located outboard of the individual wheels. *SOCIMI*

The solution adopted by Vevey Engineering for Genève in 1984 was to use the technology developed for metre-gauge railway trucks carrying standard-gauge wagons to build a trailing bogie with small wheels (375 mm diameter, compared with the standard 660 mm used in motor bogies) to support the low-floor end of one section with a suspended low-floor articulation, permitting a floor height of 480 mm over 60 per cent of the car length (there were still steps up to 870 mm over the outer motor bogies). Doorways were in the low-floor section with a folding step to give 260 + 220 mm access from street to car – not encouraging for wheelchairs. Vevey developed the concept for Bern with a similar eight-axle car on order; the motor bogies will have 560 mm diameter wheels to reduce the 'high' floor height to 710 mm, while the 'low' floor height of 350 mm over 70 per cent of the car will give 210 + 140 mm access from the street. The small wheels can be increased to 410 mm, bogie parts being accomodated under seat-carrying boxes protuding into the interior. Genève put displaced electrical equipment in cabinets within the car, but the Bern cars will move this to the roof space. The metre-gauge French system at St. Etienne has ordered cars from Vevey/Alsthom using the same principles. The problems with small wheels are increased wear, increased sensitivity to flange or rail irregularities, and increased noise. These problems can be overcome by tuning the suspension and anti-slip devices; the Vevey bogie features electro-hydraulic disk brakes, resilient wheels with rubber inserts, rubber-cone primary suspension and Flexicoil spring secondary suspension. Nevertheless some visitors to Genève have found the new cars running with noticeable flats on the small-wheel bogie giving unpleasant vibrations. A prototype of the Bern bogie with larger wheels for smoother running, and improved disc brake performance, has run 50 000 km of trials to iron out these problems.

The most successful solution requires the tramway engineer to throw away the hallowed tradition that wheels have to be connected by a rotating axle. Previous attempts to do this resulted in a proclivity for derailments, due to a lack of knowledge about the inherent physics of wheel-rail interaction, but a similar concept seems to have been proven by modern Spanish TALGO trains. The Italians were first to develop the modern tramway bogie without axles, with rebuilt prototype cars in Milano (FIREMA) and Torino (Fiat). In the latter a very short central body section rests on an unmotored bogie of torsional flexibility, with suspended articulations to the end sections. The Milano car has its Urbinati articulation cylinder as a centre section articulating between the end sections over a common articulation swivel resting on a dropped cross-beam providing rigidity between the individual wheel suspensions. Both solutions facilitate a 350 mm floor line through the articulation with the gangway lying within the bogie and longitudinal seats over the wheel intrusions.

However the similar design which has caught everyone's eye (not least for the speed with which it was developed) is that produced by Alsthom for the new system at Grenoble. Retaining 660 mm diameter wheels throughout, over 60 per cent of the car has a floor height of 345 mm, with steps up to 875 mm over the motor bogies. On a new system, all stops could be built with a 280 mm platform, permitting near level access and effective wheelchair accessibility. Again the roof space is used for displaced electrical equipment which in turn clears the workshop floor space as electrical maintenance can be carried out from gantries (and at greater intervals due to reduced ingress by dirt and contaminated water). The St Denis–Bobigny line in the Paris suburbs will use the same car, which has also attracted attention in the Netherlands.

Other designs on the drawing board take the concept even further. Kassel will be the first system to replace all the trailing bogies under a Bern-like three-section articulated car with two-wheel, axleless bogies giving the axle arrangement B'1'1'B'. Front and rear ends will be of a new design based on the profile of the Stadtbahn-N body, but with 560 mm diameter wheels in the bogies giving a 700 mm floor height. Two interior steps will lead down to a 350 mm level floor over 70 per cent of the car length, including through the articulation and EEF *(Einzelrad-Einzel-Fahrwerke)* bogies. The weight reduction through using the EEF brings the car to a very creditable 157 kg/passenger (including standing passengers at 4/m^2), compared with 250 kg/passenger for the heavy Amsterdam and Grenoble cars.

The EEF bogie has been developed by Professor Dr Ing. F Friedrich of Aachen Technical University after carefully scrutinizing the failures of experiments with pivotal bogies in the 1930s. Field tests were carried out jointly by RWTH Aachen (IFS) and Duewag, with BSI supplying forged hardware derived from heavy automotive practice. The design was tested for over 25 000 km under a Düsseldorf bogie tram and won support of a working group of undertakings and car builders (Duewag, LHB, MBB, Waggon-Union) under the auspices of the West German operators' organisation VöV for their *Stadtbahn 2000* car. In this car, which is still under development, each wheel in each bogie will be powered by an individual 60 kW motor with lateral transmission, fed via water-cooled transistor inverters compensating individual speed requirements of each wheel on curving track. The extremely compact design permits a 350 mm floor height ramping to 290 mm at doorways, with a 760 mm wide through gangway. A three-section car will have four EEF bogies (eight wheels).

Not quite so radical, and hence likely to appear first, is the MAN-GHH design for prototypes in Bremen and München, using results from a rebuilt Bremen car featuring three body sections, three bogies and freely-suspended articulations of a limited degree of rotational freedom (non-torsional), controlled by the torsion of the secondary suspension on entering a curve. The new MAN bogie features axleless wheelpairs with one off-centre, body-mounted longitudinal motor driving through a cardan shaft and a Rigiflex coupling to power two wheels in each bogie by side drive gearboxes. A disk brake is fitted to the cardan shaft. The coupling acts as a torsion shaft linking the driven wheels, but can be mounted outside the bogie frame much lower than the wheel centres. The asymmetrical weight distribution and position of the centres of rotation (there is no pivot) make this design a true modern descendant of the maximum-traction bogie

▼Full application of the EEF bogie (motored and non-motored) will come in the *Stadtbahn 2000* design being developed by German systems under VÖV sponsorship. This is the three-section version. *Drawing courtesy International Railway Journal*

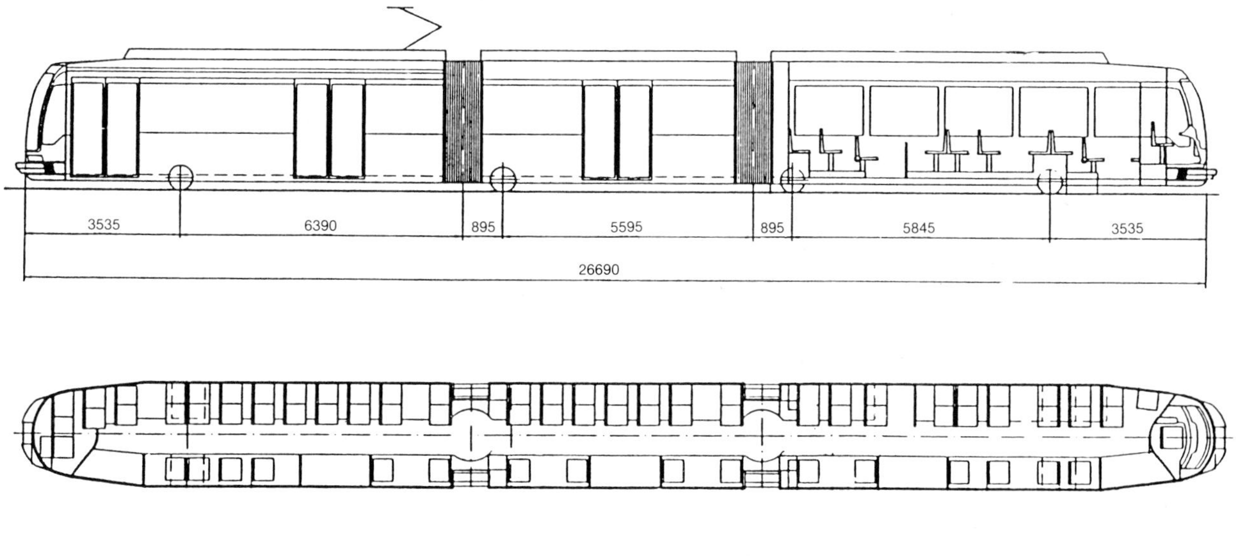

◀ Genève's light rail line 12 is now operated entirely by low-floor cars based at the new depot of Bachet-de-Pasay. Further cars are to be ordered for a second line, which will serve the main railway station at Cornavin. *M. Vieugels*

(65 per cent adhesion on the driven wheels) permitting a 350 mm through floor ramping to 300 mm at doorways. The car should achieve a weight per passenger ratio similar to the Kassel and VöV designs.

The Italians have built upon the experience with their prototypes and 54 low floor six-axle cars from Fiat-Savigliano are now entering service with ATM Torino in a smart grey, white and yellow ochre livery. Again the displaced electrical equipment has been located in the roof space. ATAC Roma has ordered 60 similar cars from SOCIMI and FIREMA are designing a prototype for Napoli. However it is SOCIMI that has taken another step forward with a speculative prototype for Milano. This is a non-articulated car with a level 350 mm floor throughout achieved by adopting a novel design of bogie. Each bogie has four 550 mm diameter independent wheels each with individual suspension and small separately-excited 20 kW motors located outboard of the wheels. Chopper equipment is microprocessor controlled with optical fibre communications. Bipolar transistors eliminate current surges and thus reduce the traditional bulky and heavy line filter. The modular concept of the car design would permit single or double-ended cars to be built, with one or two articulations. A two-section articulated car is estimated to weigh only 16.5 t. The striking design and technology of the SOCIMI prototype is certain to attract much attention.

In Great Britain the new light rail systems that are emerging are all taking the chance to use the introduction of a new mode to make the system accessible to the highest proportion of potential passengers as is possible. Indeed, guidance notes issued by the Department of Transport's Railway Inspectorate state that convenient access for the mobility impaired by a level transfer from the platform must be provided through at least one door of the LRV. This at least means the operators will not suffer the American burden of wheelchair lifts on the cars or at each stop.

Manchester with street-level access problems confined to a few stops in the city centre has developed its unique system of profiled platforms to provide level access at one door, so no low floor car design is necessary. Sheffield with its steep gradients probably needs all axles motored, but the largely street based system will require a low floor car for level boarding at all doors. Artists impressions that have been issued are not particularly relevant, since the solution will be provided by the method the successful tenderer uses to meet the specification. Birmingham have changed the car design shown in their leaflets from high-floor Nantes to low-floor Grenoble. ATA in Bristol have a link with Hawker-Siddeley, who in turn have licensing agreements with MAN.

The great shame is that there seems to be no British car builder with its own expertise to develop a standard LRV that could offer a significant cost advantage compared with licence-building small batches of adapted mainland-Europe designs. It will be interesting to see if the GEC-Alsthom merger brings Grenoble-type cars to British streets, if the Italians try to find British partners, or if the new British company formed by Hunslet with former Metro-Cammell staff to manage the Hungarian Ganz concern comes into the light rail market. Czech mass-producer Tatra is looking for customers as well.

ACKNOWLEDGEMENTS

The author is grateful for useful comments from Dr C. T. Wagner, whose own article on low-floor cars appeared in Strassenbahn Magazin 72 (1989). Other references are:
Der Stadtverkehr 2/89 "OPNV-Niederflur-Fahrzeuge im Kommen".
International Railway Journal 7/89 "Low-floor tram innovations".
Promotional literature issued by BN, MAN-GHH, Duewag, Alsthom, Vevey, Socimi, Fiat and FIREMA.

SPECIFICATION OF LOW-FLOOR LRVs

System	"Axles" motored/ total	Car length (m)	Wheel diameters (mm)	Floor height high/low (mm)	Seats/ standing	Weight (t)	Motors (kW)
Amsterdam	8/8	25.63	600	870/280	63/90	37.5	8 x 38.5
Basel	4/8	25.4	600	855/325	66/98	31	2 x 150
Würzburg	8/8	32.6	690	910/310	78/125	40	4 x 189
Genève	4/6	21	660/375	870/480	48/88	27	2 x 150
Bern	4/8	31	560/410	710/350	68/109	34	2 x 151
Torino	4/6	22.2	680	870/340	51/86	29.5	2 x 150
Grenoble	4/6	29.4	660	875/345	54/120	43.9	2 x 275
Kassel	4/6	28.75	560	700/350	80/105	29	2 x 180
VöV	3/4	26.64	750	350/290	74/79	24	6 x 60
MAN	3/6	26.8	680	350/300	67/103	25	3 x 120
SOCIMI	4/4	14	550	350	33/49	10.5	8 x 20

SOUTH YORKSHIRE LIGHT RAIL TRANSIT

Progress with 'Supertram' in Sheffield

by Paul Jackson

The proposals for a light rail or Supertram system centred on Sheffield are being promoted by the South Yorkshire Passenger Transport Executive (PTE).

The foundations of the present Supertram proposals go back to the early 1970s, when the 'Sheffield and Rotherham Land Use Transportation Study' recommended various options to meet the passenger transport requirements for the 1990s. One of these options was for a modern tramway network and sundry segregated alignments were safeguarded for a time by the then South Yorkshire County Council and Sheffield City Council.

In the early 1990s, a Segregated Passenger Transport System Working Group was instigated to firm up on proposals and assess demand in the transport corridors in question. They selected the Hillsborough and Mosborough corridors to examine in detail and numerous transport modes were investigated including Light Rail, Trolleybuses and Guided Busways coming to the conclusion that Light Rail would be the most cost effective.

Consequently, after very critical examination of the corridors and technical evaluations a Bill, entitled 'South Yorkshire Light Rail Transit Bill' was presented to Parliament in November 1985 seeking powers to construct a 25 km line from Middlewood and Stannington in the north west to Herdings/Gleadless and Halfway in the south east, passing by the railway station, through, and therefore bringing greater penetration of, the city centre. The section from Stannington to Malin Bridge was later withdrawn from the Bill at the request of the City Council. Unfortunately, the Council had not at this time given any definite commitment to the proposals and inevitably difficulties arose at the House of Commons Committee stage because of this lack of support. The proceedings were in fact adjourned on two occasions, which although creating more expense, delay and frustration for the promoters probably helped the situation be enabling the City Council to consult with the public by way of an exhibition and public meetings in September 1987 before giving its full backing subject to the following considerations:-

- That the PTE submit a second Bill in November 1988 seeking powers for Supertram route in the Lower Don Valley with the aim of regeneration of their old heavy industry area and to serve the sites for the World Student Games which are to be held in the city in July 1991.
- That if this second Bill is passed by Parliament, the depot site would be constructed in the Lower Don Valley and not at Halfway.
- That a further Bill be deposited altering the alignment at Manor Top to run along City Road.
- That subject to the Lower Don Valley Bill being passed by Parliament, the construction of Supertram routes would be re-phased so that sections of route from the city centre towards Middlewood and towards the Lower Don Valley will be operational by May 1991.

A major re-assessment study of the proposals was also commissioned at this period, due to the passage of time since the Bill was lodged and also to take in effect the complications of the de-regulation of the bus industry. This evaluation sought to answer 4 crucial questions:-

(1) Would Supertram be beneficial to Sheffield?
(2) Is there an economic case for Supertram?
(3) Would Supertram be financially viable?
(4) Would any other system confer most or all of Supertram benefits at lower cost?

The conclusion being 'Yes' to Questions 1/2/3 and 'No' to Question 4.

When the support of the City Council had been received the PTE returned to Parliament to continue the passage of the Bill, which was opposed by an Action Group, and the National Car Parks in the Commons and later by the Sheffield Chamber of Trade and a group of traders from Malin Bridge in the Lords. However, the relevant committees of MPs and Peers were satisfied with the promoter's case and rejected the opponents' petitions. Royal Assent was granted to the Bill on 27th October 1988, virtually 3 years from submission, thereby creating a precedent in current light rail proposals in that the scheme is the first to receive Royal Assent for a system based predominantly on highway rather than railway alignments.

The delay and expense occurred in the long proceedings prompted the PTE to make representations to the Joint Committee looking at Private Bill procedures in Parliament, suggesting that Public Inquiry involvement would be a better course.

As referred to previously the City Council agreed to support Supertram under certain conditions, one of which being to extend the system, through the Lower Don Valley to act as a catalyst in the regeneration of this area and to serve the 1991 World Student Games which the City had secured. The Passenger Transport Authority in February 1988 authorised the PTE to undertake a study for the section and accordingly the MVA Consultancy was commissioned to lead a study to plan cost and evaluate a route for Line 2 which would be linked to Line 1 to form a network and be capable of subsequent extension to the proposed airport at Tinsley Park and to neighbouring Rotherham.

As the target for the Bill to be submitted to Parliament was November 1988, an extremely tight timescale had to be implemented and by July the preferred alignment ran from Park Square (Junction with Line 1) alongside Cricket Inn Road crossing over on viaduct to Nunnery Sidings where the depot site is situated, alongside Woodbourn Road across Staniforth Road and alongside a canal before joining the old Great Central railway line to Tinsley. Here the line will run alongside the massive Meadowhall Shopping and Leisure Complex before terminating at the planned Meadowhall Transport Interchange. A series of public meetings and an exhibition were held and with a great deal of support, including that of the Chamber of Trade (who had objected to Line 1), the Bill was successfully lodged in Parliament. At the time of writing it has cleared the House of Lords and has received first and second readings in the Commons.

Very important developments are continuing in this district which will totally transform the severely derelict appearance, and it is worth noting that the Government established an Urban Development Corporation here with the statutory objective to secure regeneration. The support given to the Supertram proposals by this body is very encouraging, as is the backing of the developers who are involved with the Meadowhall Centre. This one complex now in the process of being built will consist of over 200 shops together with 250,000 sq ft of leisure and entertainment facilities and will consititute a major influence on the area together with the generation of a large number of public transport trips. At the Meadowhall Transport Interchange, Supertram will link in with already well advanced plans for a new British Rail station (for intercity and locally supported services) alongside a new bus station and park-and-ride facilities in addition to the 12,000 parking spaces of the Meadowhall Centre.

Of course, financing the project is a major stage of its development and therefore during December 1988, the PTE applied to the Department of Transport for Capital Allocation and Section 56 grant towards the capitalised cost of Line 1. The Transport Minister, Mr Portillo, has authorised a 50% grant towards further development work on Line 1. Satisfactory reports will hopefully result in the necessary approvals. The PTE has also applied for grant towards the cost of Line 2, subject to receiving powers being sought in Parliament.

The Department of Transport have said they expect the PTE "to develop sound proposals for ... financing, and to secure contributions from the private sector – particularly the interests along the route which will benefit from the project." It seems likely that the system will operate through a 'Concessionaire' concept which will contain the required private sector element. The Concessionaire may let contracts for the operation and maintenance of the system. Seemingly, the Concessionaire will also be responsible for the construction of the scheme and for the subsequent performance of its operation and maintenance. In this respect Supertram differs significantly from the Greater Manchester 'Design, Build and Operate & Maintain' approach.

Although the design of the vehicles is still under review, certain details have emerged. There will be around 25 vehicles required for Lines 1 and 2, each being probably betwen 30 and 40 metres long with a crush load capacity of up to 250 and up to 100 seats. The vehicles will be up to 2.65 metres wide and fully accessible by those passengers whose mobility is impaired. The importance of this will ensure the floor height at doorways and over as much of the vehicles as possible is close to the kerb heights at stops. Severe gradients encountered in Sheffield will, however, rule out solutions which use unpowered bogies. On-street, the vehicles will operate strictly in accordance with the prevailing highway

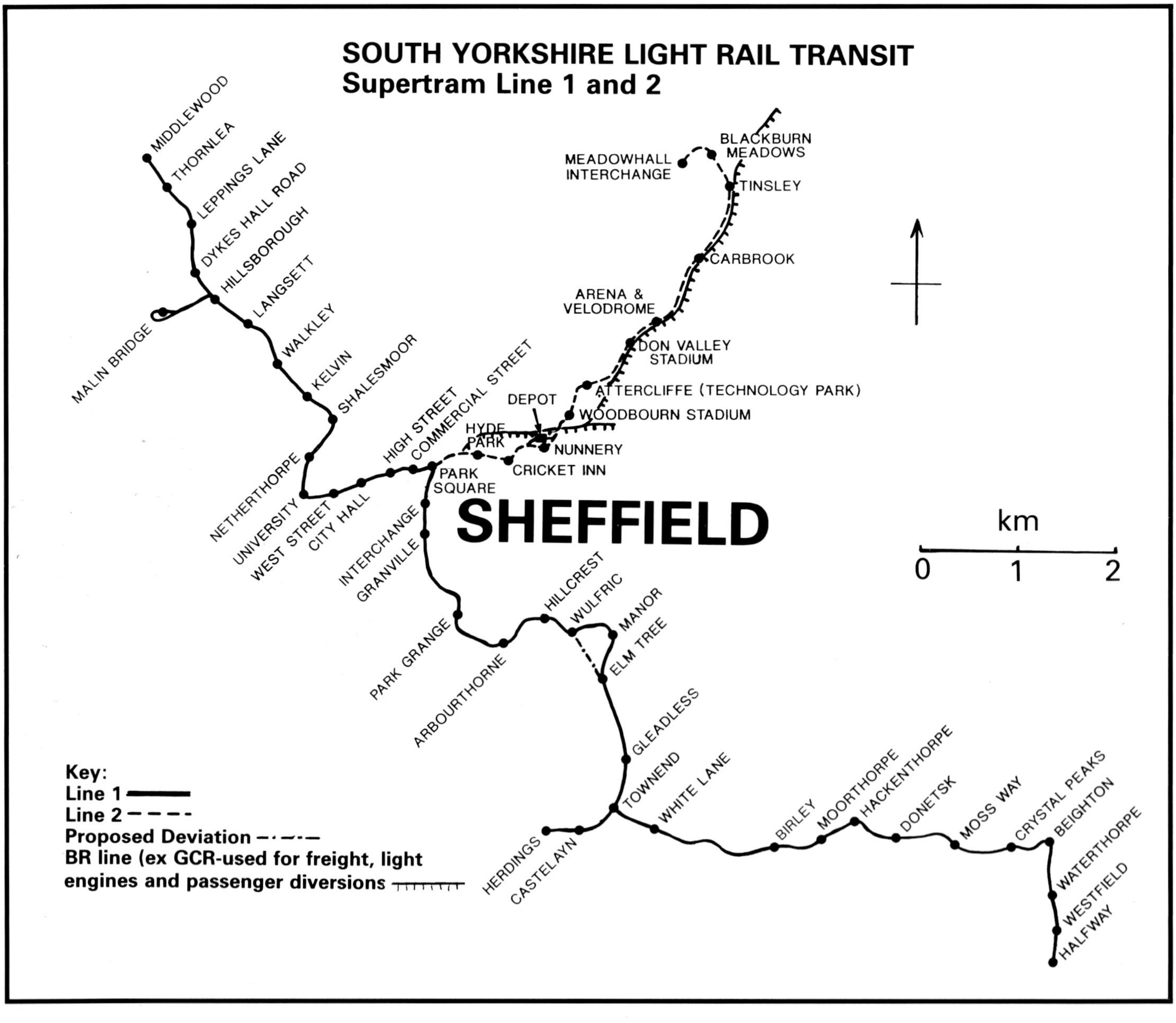

speed limits . However, on segregated track maximum speed will be 50 mph (80 km/h). It is not envisaged that drivers will sell or check tickets, but there will be a team of 'revenue protection staff' to enforce whatever form of self-service ticketing is developed.

Lines 1 and 2 have always been seen as part of a wider network and it is understood that Barnsley, Doncaster and Rotherham Councils would welcome extensions into their respective areas. Design factors therefore are needed urgently to be universally applicable.

On Line 1 approximately half of the route will be laid in the form of a tramway with grooved rail, but where sufficient carriageway exists it is proposed to operate along a tram lane laid slightly above the general level as in Amsterdam. At all stops passengers will load directly from platforms, kerbs or islands, and therefore there will be no problems by having to board amongst other road traffic.

It is intended that priority will be given to Supertram on-street and at highway crossings, through new traffic light controlled junctions. In certain streets in the City Centre other traffic is already limited to buses and access only and it is possible that the City Council will introduce similar traffic regulations to other sections of the route.

The PTE is currently aspiring to open a key section of the route from the Lower Don Valley to the City Centre by 1991 to coincide with the World Student Games. Construction of the remainder of Line 1 would follow with completion by 1993.

Advertisements inviting companies to register their interest in tendering for design and build contracts were placed in the press in September 1988 and shortlisting of respondents has taken place. In September 1989, similar advertisements were placed relating to operating and maintenance contracts.

In conclusion it is considered that Supertram will offer great benefit for the City of Sheffield by improving accessibility to the City Centre and new employment possibilities for local residents, importantly including those whose mobility is impaired. It will enhance the prestige and create a modern image for the City and hopefully in time to other parts of South Yorkshire.

In the recently released 'Sheffield Development Corporation Lower Don Valley Regeneration Strategy Report' an interesting item appears suggesting that a traditional tramway could provide a short high frequency public transport route between the City Centre (Canal Basin) and a suggested new British Rail station midway between Sheffield and Meadowhall railway stations at Newhall serving the north side of the Lower Don Valley away from the Supertram Line 2 route. It would provide access to major development sites for up to 5,000 employees with the opportunity to reduce car parking provision. The tramway could become a tourist attraction to promote the Lower Don Valley both within the City and elsewhere.

This suggestion shows that the 'heritage tramway' concept is gaining respect within the United Kingdom and can complement light rail developments.

Because of the fact that the road which formed the original route of Supertram line 1 through the Manor Estate is not now to be widened, a diversion has been proposed along City Road. This artists impression shows a car in City Road near Manor Top. Note the change in texture of the road surface in the area where parking is allowed. *South Yorkshire PTE*

PHOTO FEATURE

Light Rail in the USA

SAN DIEGO, CALIFORNIA

▲San Diego led the US light rail boom with its low-cost line linking the city with the Mexican border, achieving farebox ratios in excess of 80%. The city terminus is on protected street track at the Santa Fe railway station. *J. Wolinsky*

◄The San Diego Trolley took over a railway with residual traffic for its light rail alignments. Freight trains still run at night, but the trestle has been rebuilt for double track. *F.W. Schneider III*

►The success of the first line in San Diego has prompted a second to serve the Eastern suburbs. This view shows a single Siemens/Duewag car at Euclid. *F.W. Schneider III*

BUFFALO, NEW YORK

▲The surface light rail line is the centre piece of a new city centre mall in Buffalo. The line enters a subway under a congested suburban highway.

M. Vieugels

SACRAMENTO, CALIFORNIA

▲Sacramento diverted funds from an unfinished freeway to finance light rail construction. Part of the 1987 line is built on the abandoned highway alignment. *F.W. Schneider III*

►A second line in Sacramento uses some clever civil engineering to weave a single-track section under an elevated highway and across the adjacent railway. *F.W. Schneider III*

▼Street track is also used in Sacramento, with lining to discourage motor vehicle trespass. The Siemens–Duewag LRVs, originally developed for Frankfurt, are also found in San Diego and Pittsburgh. *F.W. Schneider III*

SHAKER HEIGHTS, OHIO

▲The Shaker Heights lines in Cleveland, USA, are a model light rail operation, substantially modernised in the last decade, with new LRVs from Breda. Suburban station feature park-and-ride facilities. *F.W. Schneider III*

SAN JOSE, CALIFORNIA

▲Another new Californian light rail line has been built at San Jose. In the city centre a so-called transit mall permits access by private car as well as a protected alignment for light rail. *F.W. Schneider III*

►On the edge of the central district a short underpass takes the San Jose light rail line under the Los Angeles–Seattle railway. *F.W. Schneider III*

▼In the suburbs the San Jose line is located on ballasted reservation. The articulated cars were built in Canada by UTDC (a Lavalin subsidiary). *F.W. Schneider III*

PITTSBURGH, PA

▲Pittsburgh's suburban lines feature a mixture of street and reserved track. The Siemens–Duewag LRVs have one entrance with steps for street operation, and high floors for platforms at stations. *F.W. Schneider III*

.SEVERANCE PAYS OFF

Manchester Spearheads the Light Rail Revolution

by David Holt

INTRODUCTION

Most public works projects require members of several different professions to work closely together, few more so than Manchester's Metrolink LRT scheme. As well as the wide range of directly-involved disciplines, the number of outside bodies which have to be consulted is phenomenal. They include the local police, the highway authorities, ten District Councils, the Department of Transport, various statutory undertakings, the local business community, British Rail, HM Railway Inspectorate, the fire brigade, the Urban Traffic Control Unit, the electricity supplier, user groups, property owners and tenants, the unions and, of course, the general public.

Compound this with the monumental ignorance about light rail which exists amongst the British public, add the awkwardness of the present British legislative system, and you have a pretty challenging set of circumstances. And as if that were not enough, it is clear that whatever is done in Manchester will establish a whole range of precedents for following LRT schemes. On top of all this HM Government is imposing on Metrolink the burden of testing an unproven form of implementation contract.

In this added aggravation of such a trailblazing project there is a cruel irony. Metrolink is being designed to welcome aboard mobility-impaired people, giving them equality with other passengers. This is being done by careful design and by getting rid of obstacles to movement; yet obstacles have repeatedly confronted the scheme itself. In a caring nation one would think that such a scheme would be championed as an example for others to follow; instead its every step forward is being handicapped in some way. Metrolink, as we shall see later, has in a way suffered the ordeal of a creature which has its legs pulled off one at a time by a child curious to see whether it can still make forward progress.

PREPARATORY WORK

Thanks to the perseverance of the scheme's promoters, there is now some real physical evidence of progress. With an October 1989 contract start date in view, the underground plant of various statutory bodies – water, gas, electricity, telephones and so on – is being ducted or re-located so that future access to it is not impeded by the presence of the light rail tracks.

These activities cover just about the entire extent of Metrolink in the city centre. Even though they involve prodigious roadworks there has been no great traffic chaos or public outcry; this is surely a tribute to competent management and good public relations and augurs well for tolerance of tracklaying work when it takes place soon.

Here and there dotted lines recently appeared showing the path of the tracks through the streets; this was done by the city's highway engineers to guide the services re-location teams. In addition, the outline of the inbound platform in High Street was marked out and identified at either end with the word "platform" in large letters on the flagstones – giving a gentle hint of something more solid to follow shortly.

PROFILED PLATFORMS

The platform thus outlined will be one of four or five in the city centre built to a design exclusive to Metrolink. To appreciate what is involved one must understand the unique nature of the proposed LRT system. Phase 1 will make use of 22 high-platformed stations, 19 of them ex British Rail, as well as the crucial few on-street stations. Originally it had been proposed to use vehicles with folding steps able to load either at high platforms or from kerb level, but things became more complicated when a decision was taken to make the system fully disabled-friendly.

After looking at various options a solution was arrived at which is uniquely Manchester's. Conventional high-floored LRVs will be used, and this has widened the choice of vehicles by making use of simple and well-proven LRV designs and technology; flat floors throughout the interiors of the vehicles will also mean greater passenger safety and convenience. At the 22 high-platformed stations, level access will be available at all doorways in a train, which may consist of a maximum of two articulated units; there will be no need for disruptive and expensive alterations to the levels of existing station platforms.

At St Peters Square and High Street/Market Street, where because of environmental sensitivity and lack of space high platforms cannot at present be sanctioned, some means had to be found to allow disabled people to board and alight; these two stops will be amongst the most popular destinations on the entire system. And so it is here that Manchester's specially-developed solution – 'profiled platforms' – will be applied. The form that these will actually take differs from the illustration in that the raised portion will be longer and will serve the centremost LRV entrances, a modification proposed by the GMA consortium.

The remaining LRV doorways, equipped with single retracting steps, will be accessed from long low-height platforms at approximately double kerb level. Changes in height will be accomplished longitudinally by means of ramps and laterally by means of steps. To facilitate pedestrian movement, each profiled platform will be equipped with pedestrian crossing and access facilities part way along its length. The accompanying drawings illustrate the principles.

DESIGN CONSIDERATIONS

These prominent on-street stations will be crucial to the impact of Metrolink on Manchester. The reaction with which Manchester folk greet LRT will be much conditioned by its appearance; ugly structures and brutal-looking vehicles would fuel hostility, whereas a generally friendly and agreeable aspect will ease acceptance. It is also necessary to confer a corporate identity or system-wide image on Metrolink so that people will instantly recognise anything which forms part of it.

The design process revolves essentially around the harmonisation of engineering and aesthetics within a constrained

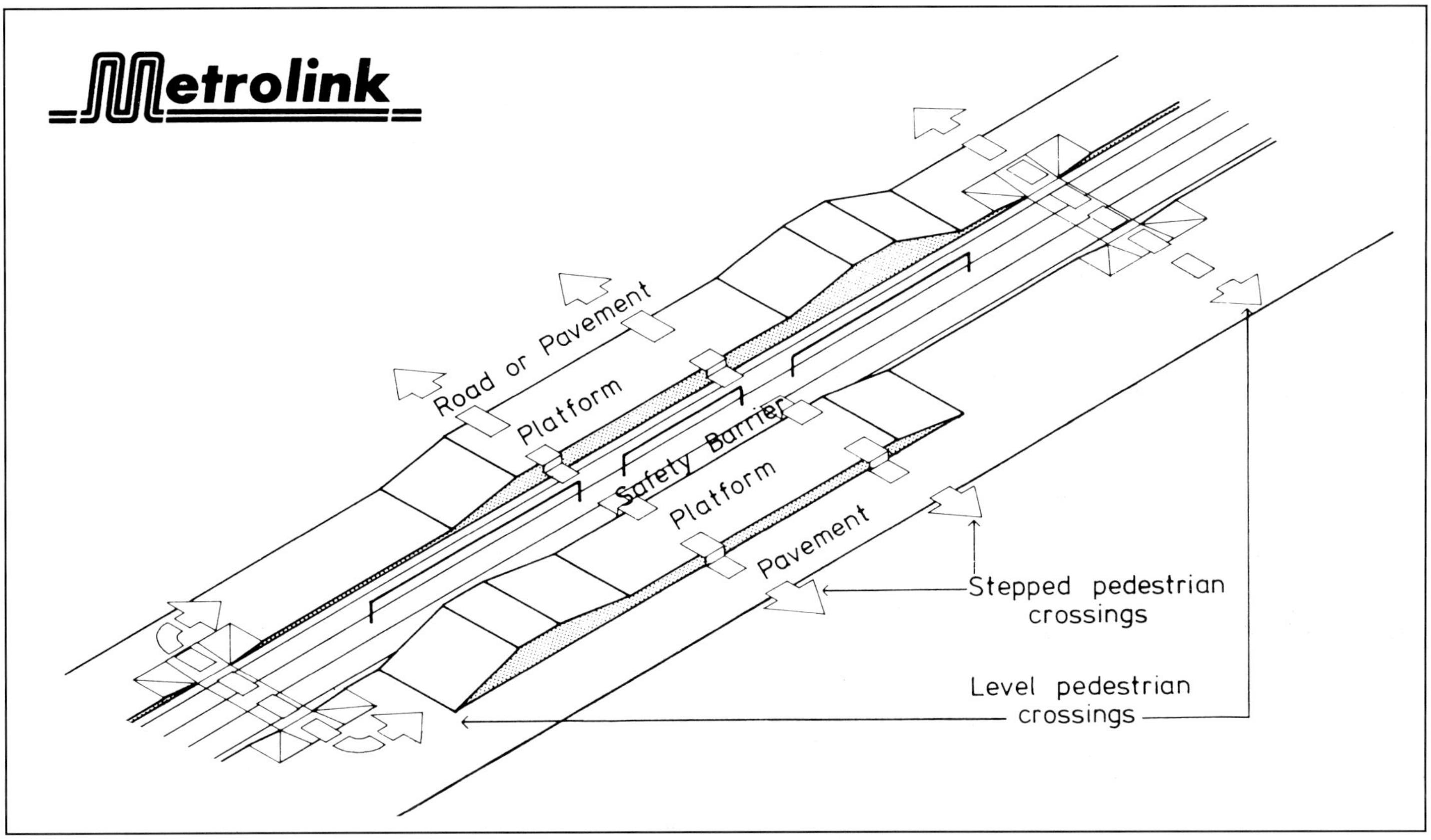

▲The general layout of the METROLINK profiled platforms which will be used in three city centre stations.

◀Position of retractable step to platform.

◀▼Pedestrian safety barrier at the rear of the high level section of the platform.

▼Route of METROLINK through Central Manchester showing locations of stations.

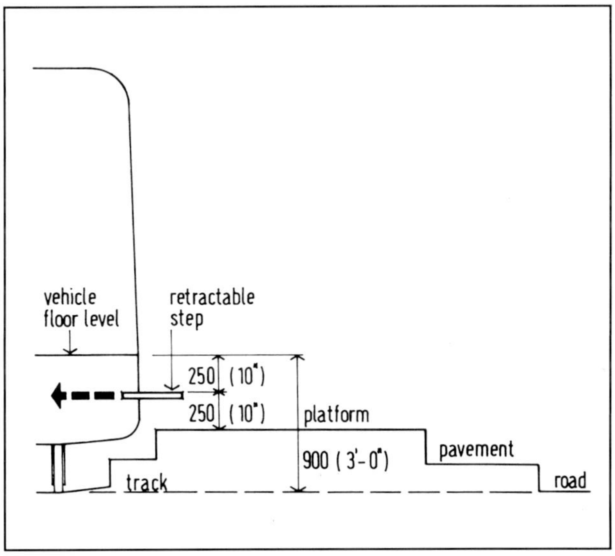

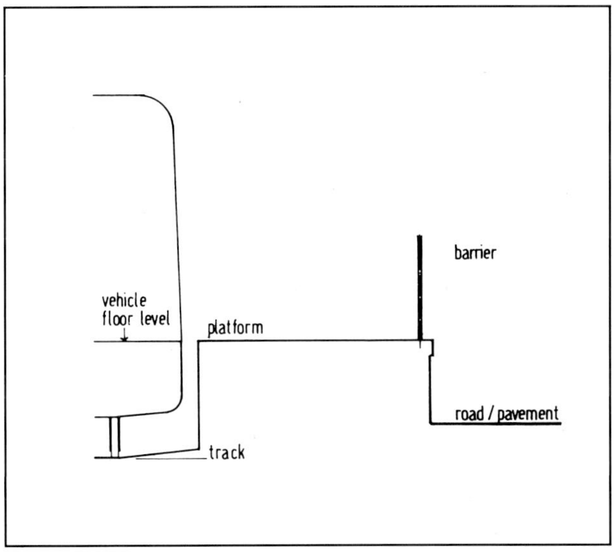

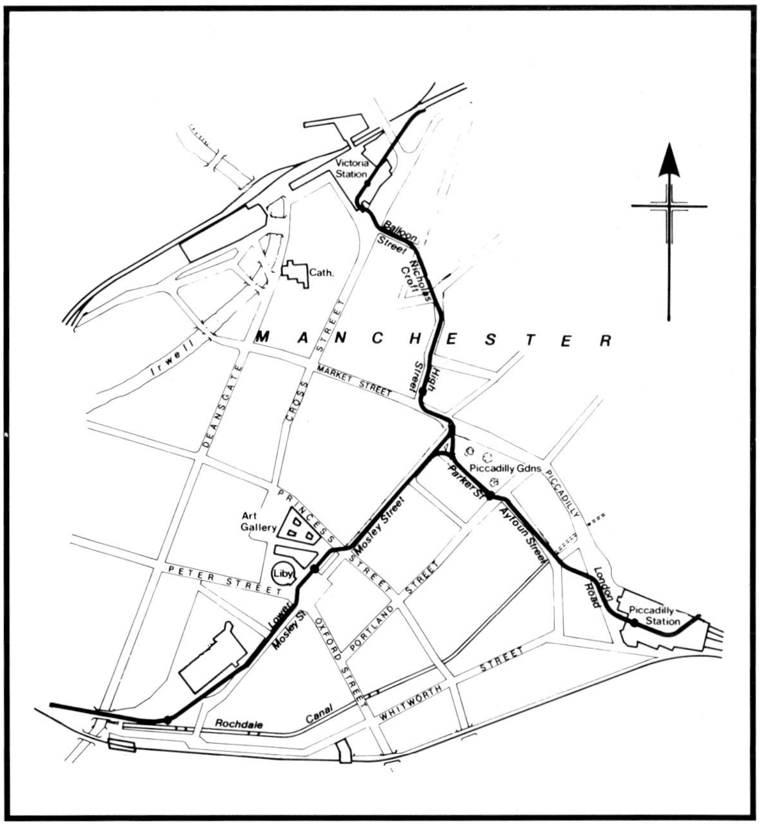

Artist's impression of the METROLINK scheme. The impression above shows an LRV leaving Bury Transport Interchange on ex-BR alignment (with the unique 1200 V dc side contact third rail used by the present trains still in place!).

The view below shows an LRV running through St. Peters Square in the centre of Manchester. A second LRV can be seen standing at the proposed station.

▶The Birchfields Road mock-up in November 1988, clearly showing the raised section of the profiled platform. *D. Holt*

▼This existing doorway will be enlarged to enable LRVs to run into Piccadilly undercroft LRT station from London Road. Metrolink preparatory work can be seen in the foreground in this June 1989 view. *D. Holt courtesy TMS archives*

Mosley Street at its junction with Market Street in June 1989, with Metrolink preparatory work in full swing. *D. Holt, courtesy TMS archives*

budget. This is no easy task, and to help explain what is involved the author can do no better than quote from a paper given to a conference by Mr Tom Parkinson of Canada:

"*...This 'lightness' of light rail, a combination of flexibility, low impact, modest cost and environmental softness, is ephemeral. It must be carefully guarded. Ignorance or ineptitude during the planning, design, specification writing, engineering or construction phases of a project can lose the 'lightness'. Light rail's advantages can be diminished or even destroyed with overdesigned overhead, ugly, noisy or difficult to maintain cars, poorly conceived alignments or simply uneconomic applications. This is why certain systems provide better examples of Light Rail's 'lightness'...*"

Throughout the development of Manchester's light rail project these principles have been rigidly adhered to. The mysterious forces which seem to have drawn other LRT schemes down into tunnels or up into the air have been firmly resisted here. As originally conceived, Metrolink will be well integrated at ground level into the rational lifestyle of a city which refuses to banish people from its surface.

Fundamental to the vitality of Manchester's light rail proposals has been continuous all-party local support. The policies behind the proposals were embodied in the County Structure Plan and they survived the abolition of the Greater Manchester Council and the establishment of the new Passenger Transport Authority in 1986. It is the business of the Passenger Transport Executive to see such policies through to fruition; to which end various other agencies have been brought to bear.

METROLINK PROJECT GROUP

Within the PTE a Metrolink Project Group was set up last year effectively to take over Phase 1 of the LRT scheme from the PTE Planning Office and to see it through to completion; matters concerning later phases remain the remit of the PTE's Planning Officers until the time comes for their implementation.

ENGINEERING CONSULTANCY

As it is out of the question for a PTE to retain in-house all the expertise needed to design and implement a new state-of-the-art LRT system, normal practice is to engage outside specialists to work on the more detailed aspects. At a very early stage in the formulation of the LRT proposals the services of engineering consultants were engaged – in this case Mott, Hay and Anderson (now Mott Macdonald). The PTA and PTE knew broadly what they required, but had to have expert advice on the engineering feasibility of various options including, as possible alternatives, public transport modes other than light rail. Financial, environmental impact, vehicle design and other consultation has also been undertaken as well as dialogues with the wide range of outside bodies referred to earlier.

Following on from the feasibility studies, the engineering consultants proceeded to put flesh on the bare bones of the chosen light rail proposals. One important task which they undertook was to look into various possible forms of contract, together with contract supervision – which conventionally would be left in the hands of the engineering consultants themselves.

The consultants' recommendation was that the best way forward would be by means of a 'Design and Build' form of contract, similar in outline to that which was used to construct the Docklands Light Railway. It was on that basis that the PTE proceeded, until they were audaciously instructed otherwise by the Government. The contract now includes, at the Government's rather whimsical insistence, operation and maintenance of the system. The form of light rail contract this entails – design, build, operate and maintain – has never before met with success on this planet, so it is small wonder that its imposition inflicts major headaches. Nevertheless, progress continues to be made.

THE DESIGN CHALLENGE

To introduce the concept of street-running LRT design, it may be helpful to draw an analogy with a well-known feature of our streets – the telephone kiosk. As something which provides a useful public service, phone kiosks are put in the street because that is where they are most publicly available. Here we have an exact parallel with LRT; the more exposed and available it is, the more successful it will be in advertising itself and being well used, but – the greater will be the design challenge.

British Telecom's new phone kiosks are distinctive in appearance and at the same time unobtrusive. When you want one, they're easy to spot – and when you don't, you're not especially aware of them. That is how it has to be with surface LRT in an established city centre.

An important element of any transport system is the sort of image which it presents to the public. A central quality of mixed-alignment LRT is its flexibility, which also makes it perhaps the toughest single mode on which to confer a distinctive system-wide image. London Transport had this sort of problem when it was formed in 1933; in that case one common image had to be applied to a system embodying many different modes of transport. The brilliant circle-and-bar logo, inherited from the Underground Group, remains with us today as the unique and easily-recognised symbol of public transport in the capital.

In the case of Metrolink, the common image has to be applied in a diversity of situations ranging from city-centre streets to suburban railway stations. Fixed equipment, structures and vehicles all have to reflect, and contribute to, the desired system-wide image. This image has to be a subtle blend of friendliness and assertiveness as well as inconspicuousness and 'presence'. To hit the right note demands intimate local knowledge as well as a sound understanding of the nature of light rail.

In Manchester the portfolio of a local practice – EGS Design – made them the PTE's natural choice. Amongst many local projects which the firm has to its credit, the GMEX exhibition centre and the Bury and Altrincham bus/rail interchanges are particularly relevant. The latter two projects entailed close co-operation with the PTE and with British Rail, the former with the City Council.

The brief given to EGS by the PTE was not a narrow one, including as it did all aspects of the system's design from lettering to colour schemes and from architectural compatibility to passenger flow. In a nutshell, EGS have used as a starting point the engineering fundamentals of LRT and have then set out to make sure that the system will sit acceptably and successfully in a mature cosmopolitan and commercial centre.

SUCCESS

The Metrolink proposals are now poised on the threshold of realisation. After a long and very painstaking two-stage tender evaluation process, the PTE announced on 27th September that the GMA Consortium's tender to design, build, operate and maintain Metrolink had been selected on cost and several other grounds. GMA has a strong local content as well as a very solid background of experience; it is instructive to note in passing that this consortium demonstrated rather more concern for the system's enhanced accessibility than did the other contenders.

Four firms make up GMA – they are GEC, Mowlem, AMEC, and GM Buses. GEC Transportation Projects Limited will bring to Metrolink its international expertise in light railway systems, and John Mowlem & Company PLC will contribute worldwide experience in all forms of construction work; together these two firms already form the GEC–Mowlem Railway Group which achieved so much success on the pioneering Docklands Light Railway project. Fairclough Civil Engineering, the division of AMEC which will be involved in Metrolink, has considerable local railway and other construction experience. Interestingly enough, just before the emergence of Manchester's LRT proposals in 1983 Faircloughs helped with the successful unearthing and rescue of 62 tons of Salford tramway junction from the path of the M602 motorway extension. This is not without a small degree of significance in the present context.

The operator member of the winning consortium could hardly be more appropriate. GM Buses currently runs a fleet of over 2000 vehicles in and around the Greater Manchester region as well as having within itself a great wealth of local public transport experience with which to benefit Metrolink.

All the people who have worked so hard over the last few years were rewarded on 24th October. On that momentous day, Mr Michael Portillo, Minister of State for Transport, announced that the government would make a grant under Section 56 of the Transport Act 1968 available to cover 50% of the scheme's £110 million eligible costs, the remainder to be funded by the PTA.

A letter of intent has now gone from the PTE to GMA, contract documentation is being drafted and the implementation program is gathering momentum. Detailed design work is under way and a mock-up LRV will be delivered early in the new year by FIREMA, the Italian firm which is to build the vehicles.

Work on-street is expected to start in springtime at Victoria station and will be carried on in parallel with other works.

By virtue of widespread local support, judicious project management, a high degree of professionalism and a complete understanding of light rail, the PTE and PTA are guaranteeing the people of Manchester an LRT system designed to the highest possible standards – as we shall soon discover. The next two years are going to be, to say the very least, exciting.

Metrolink

SOLUTIONS....

Metrolink

Metrolink

Public transportation systems

by applying Fairclough Technology

In more than a century of progress Fairclough has become a major force in civil engineering by continuously evolving and adapting to meet marketplace demands.

It takes challenges in its stride and provides solutions. By the application of design, engineering and project management expertise. By constantly investing in high-tech equipment and highly-skilled people.

By calling on the resources of parent group AMEC plc, one of the largest construction and engineering concerns in Britain.

By playing a part in the **GMA Group's** solution to the easing of urban congestion throughout Greater Manchester in the design, construction and operation of the pioneering £90M **Metrolink LRT system,** as conceived by the **Greater Manchester Passenger Transport Authority.**

Fairclough

Fairclough Civil Engineering Limited
Chapel Street, Adlington, Lancashire PR7 4JP. Telephone: (0257) 480264 · Telex: 67510 · Fax: (0257) 481801
The AMEC Group

Metrolink

COLOUR FEATURE

LRT Around the World

BASEL, SWITZERLAND

▲The centre of Basel, Switzerland, is virtually traffic-free, permitting high-quality surface public transport that runs to timetables you can set your watch by. As a result patronage is booming. *M.R. Taplin*

◄The suburban light rail lines in Basel are an example of how a frequent and reliable service can be provided using single-track and loops to minimise infrastructure land take. *R.N.H. Jones*

THE RUHR, GERMANY

▲The German Stadtbahn-B LRV design is standard to several systems in Nordrhein–Westfalen, including the linked examples in the Ruhr conurbation. This Dortmund car serves only high platforms, but others have folding steps for street operation.
J.F. Bromley

ROMANIA

►Romania has opened six new light rail systems in the last decade as part of its programme to boost electric city transport. This colourful example is at Cluj–Napoca.
Earl W. Clark

TUNIS

▼Light rail systems are being installed in several developing countries where large numbers of passengers need to be moved efficiently, but funding precludes a full metro. The most ambitious project is in Tunis, financed by Austrian and German banks.
R.N.H. Jones

HONG KONG

▲Hong Kong has a traditional tramway with the British tradition of double-deck cars developed for local conditions. These have been rebodied since 1986 while consideration is given to rolling stock design for the future. *M.R. Taplin*

◀In 1988 a new light rail system was opened in Hong Kong, based on Tuen Mun in the New Territories. Intensive services were operated on the network using large bogie cars built in Australia by Commonwealth Engineering. *R.N.H. Jones*

MELBOURNE, AUSTRALIA

▼The largest system in the southern hemisphere, Melbourne, is buying 130 articulated cars and converting lightly-used suburban railways to light rail operation. *M.R. Taplin*

TORONTO, CANADA

▲In Toronto a largely street-based tramway network is operated in traditional North American fashion, but recent investment in new rolling stock, including 42 articulated cars, is now being matched by new extensions built to light rail standards.

J.F. Bromley

USA

►Los Angeles, the city that tried to adapt to unlimited car traffic, is now promoting a switch to public transport. Two light rail lines are under construction and the first car arrived in 1989. *J. Wolinsky*

▼The Shaker Heights lines in Cleveland, USA, are a model light rail operation, substantially modernised in the last decade, with new LRVs from Breda. Suburban stations feature park-and-ride facilities.

James Smith

KARLSRUHE
Public Transport Showpiece

by Jack Wyse

INTRODUCTION

The West German city of Karlsruhe is situated in the upper Rhein plain on the northern fringe of the Black Forest and was one of a group of towns originally built to a geometric plan by the prince builders of southern Germany. The city developed alongside the palace of Prince Karl Wilhelm, which remains the hub of the central street layout, and the present main railway station of 1913 (a through station replacing a cramped 1843 terminus) had to be built some 1.5 km from the city centre, Marktplatz, a factor which accounts for the light rail developments described in this article. Although badly damaged in the war, the city has been restored and retains an attractive historic central area, which has been a strong incentive for the community to adopt a planning strategy avoiding reliance on private motoring, and maximising the use of public transport.

The city has a population approaching 290 000, but is the regional centre for 400 000 inhabitants. It is an important industrial centre (though industry is kept well to the west of the city towards the river Rhein and its harbour), a very large nuclear research centre is built in forest well to the north of the city (but served by the latest light rail extension), the oldest technical university in Germany lies just off the central area, and the city is the home of the highest Federal courts. The working population is drawn from a wide area of small towns and villages, mostly served by rail links provided by the Federal Railways (DB) or by the City Council through its transport company (VBK) or light rail subsidiary (AVG).

Although the number of private cars is still increasing (by 3.6% in 1986, to 520 cars per 1000 population, with 70% of households car-owning), new roads cannot be planned, let alone built, quite apart from land use considerations. The search for alternatives to the motor car is becoming a matter for emergency measures. In Karlsruhe all the political parties are united in believing that only public transport improvements relieve the pressure on road space, reduce noise and emission of pollutants, and improve the quality of life in the densely-populated areas. A major effort to change the modal split in favour of public transport has already achieved a 50% balance in the central area, and is now concentrated on improving the suburban ratio from 10% public transport – 90% private to a 30:70 split by increasing the speed of public transport.

While public transport use throughout West Germany fell by one% in 1988, in the Karlsruhe area it rose by 3.1%. The official reason for the national drop is a fall in the school-age population and increased private motoring. The cause of the reverse trend in Karlsruhe is an improvement in the quality and capacity of public transport, together with the introduction of low-cost ride-at-will tickets which everyone finds so easy to buy and use. Almost 40% of passengers use the freely-transferable environmental season ticket (DM 43 per month or DM 430 per annum payable by monthly direct debit), while many of the others use the 24-hour family tickets (two adults and up to four children) costing only DM 5 in the city or DM 10 in the region. One in four households in Karlsruhe is estimated to have a public transport season ticket of some kind.

THE ALBTALBAHN

Thirty two years ago the city took over from a private company a worn-out 40-km metre-gauge electric light railway running south through the suburban community of Ettlingen to the Black Forest towns of Bad Herrenalb and Ittersbach.

◄The Black Forest community of Ittersbach campaigned long and hard for the restoration of its rail link to Karlsruhe, achieving success in 1975 when the Albtalbahn extension was opened. *M.R. Taplin*

►▲The Albtalbahn was designed for mixed operation of light rail and heavy rail, the latter including both freight operation and tourist trains. Herrenalb is the location as a service car meets a preserved steam-hauled DB Class ET 25 museum EMU. *C.T. Wagner*

►The Albtalbahn has its own tree-lined reservation alongside the main road south from Karlsruhe, and carries heavy suburban traffic. *M.R. Taplin*

It was decided to convert the system to standard-gauge and integrate it with the city tramways to permit through running to the central area, eliminating a change at the Albtalbahnhof for thousands of passengers daily. The conversion began in 1958, and was mostly completed by 1960, although re-extension to Ittersbach did not come until 1975. Modern articulated light rail vehicles offered improved journey times (including express runs at peak periods) and featured multiple-unit operation south of the Albtalbahnhof. Interestingly, freight traffic was worth retaining, a DB connection at Ettlingen and a daily diesel freight service to 11 private sidings shifts 70 000 tonnes each year. It also permits preserved steam locomotives to provide a tourist service on some summer Sundays.

▲The Albtalbahn south of Karlsruhe carries heavy commuter traffic, but is also an important tourist link with Black Forest resorts, benefitting off-peak loadings. This scene shows the station at Marxzell. *M.R. Taplin*

Through running of trams and trains was to be the foundation for the future development of light rail services around Karlsruhe. Once standard-gauge light rail cars were required to share tracks with railway vehicles, it was necessary to design a wheel profile for the light rail cars which was compatible with both railway (EBO) and tramway (BOStrab) requirements, and this was the key to successful further development. The special wheel profile had to be able to negotiate railway pointwork without derailing, but the wheel-deflecting plates of this pointwork had to be raised 10 mm where light rail services operate. On the other hand DB rolling stock had to be able to use the joint track without having to be modified in any way, although in practice the locomotives carry AVG communications equipment. The light rail cars have to carry magnetic track brakes and be able to negotiate 25-metre radius curves on the urban tram routes, and have to carry appropriate safety equipment, including Indusi and air-whistles to meet railway regulations.

►At Busenbach on the Albtalbahn the branch to Ittersbach diverges from the main line to Herrenalb at a signal-controlled junction. *A.P.H. Velthoen*

►Traffic on Karlsruhe's east-west public transport axis is growing, requiring multiple-unit operation of articulated cars. *M. Brosteaux*

◄Wörth is planned to be the second destination for dual voltage light rail vehicles which can run on DB tracks. The local service from Karlsruhe is at present provided by new Class 628.2 DMUs. *Peter Fox*

THE HARDTBAHN

In 1975 an urban tramway extension was built to serve the new housing area of Nordweststadt. The adjacent community of Neureut (beyond the city boundary) had had its own urban bus service since 1950, but passengers had neither a through service nor a through fare to Karlsruhe. An indirect DB line ran through Neureut en route from Leopoldshafen and Eggenstein to Karlsruhe via Knielingen, but this had been freight-only since 1967 because of falling numbers of passengers, discouraged by the long detour to the Hauptbahnhof (Hbf), where it was necessary to change to trams (and buy another ticket) for the city centre. In 1979 Neureut was incorporated within the city boundary, and got its through tram service at the same time by an extension from Nordweststadt that ran over part of the DB freight line.

The DB line ran right through the built-up area of Neureut, and its incorporation into the Stadtbahn was a result of close collaboration between DB and VBK (working through AVG, since the service was provided by extending Albtalbahn services across the city to Neureut). DB remained the owner of the rail line, while VBK undertook to ensure compatibility and carry out all necessary maintenance. Because railway regulations (EBO) still applied to use of the DB track, use was made of AVG, which had the experience and trained personnel to provide the service. The joint DB-AVG section had a length of 1.5 km, and the necessary signalling equipment was put under the remote control of the AVG central signalbox in Ettlingen.

The link with DB was important because it provided the basis for further extension of the Hardtbahn (as the northern route was called). The next section was opened from Neureut to Eggenstein and Leopoldshafen-Nord on 13 December 1986, following pressure from the local communities which began almost as soon as the Neureut extension was built. Much of this line beyond Neureut followed the DB freight line, and only within Leopoldshafen was it necessary to build a new light rail alignment to provide a service in close proximity to the residential area. The entire public transport network in the Unter Hardt area was reorganised at the same time, affecting the bus services of VBK and AVG, and giving the travelling public an integrated fare system. Traffic on the Stadtbahn increased by 73% compared with that on the previous bus services.

The introduction of a new 9-km privately owned (i.e. non-DB) railway led to new arrangements between AVG and DB. AVG took over the track and foundations from DB; DB retained the right to continue running the same level of freight traffic indefinitely at its own expense. All platform heights were 380 mm to permit the continued passage of

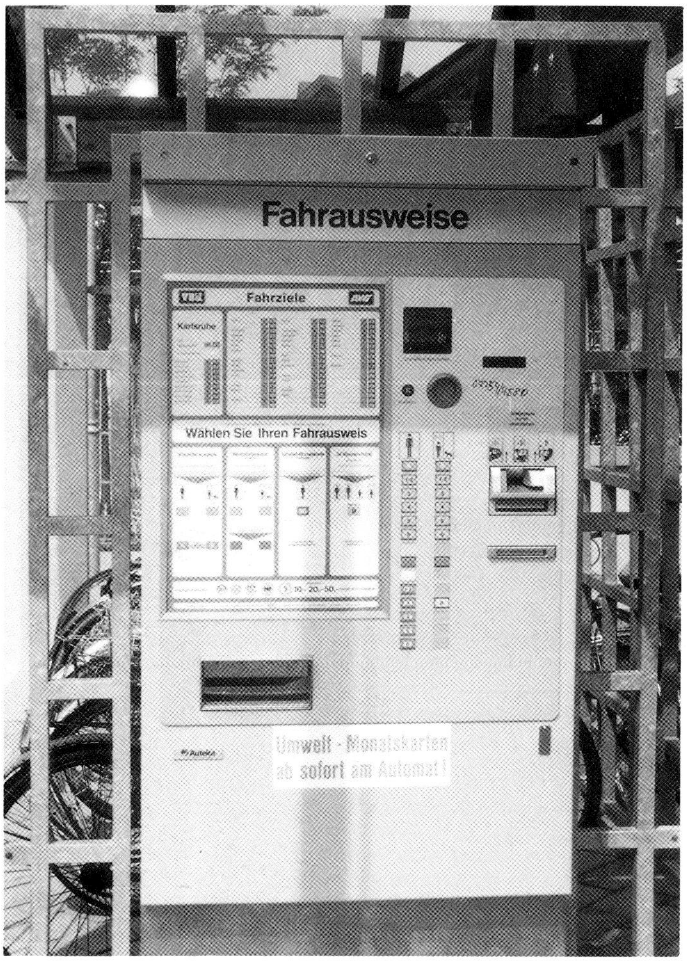

railway vehicles. The whole 9 km were signalled to railway standards and controlled by AVG from Ettlingen. In order to protect two types of vehicle, Indusi magnetic barrier protection at stop signals is actuated by protective devices on the light rail cars, while conventional 2000 Hz magnets provide protection for DB vehicles. A 15-km optical-fibre link with a band width from 2 Hz to 7.5 MHz connects Neureut with Ettlingen signalbox. In addition to signalling data, this also carries radio, loudspeaker information and clock-control signals. The former single track was doubled over 1 km lengths in both Neureut and Eggenstein, both loops covering two stops so as to permit cars to pass at speed without the delay of waiting at stops.

The new alignment through the centre of Leopoldshafen ran close to homes so that noise-shielding had to be provided; this took the form of sound-absorbing material under the ballast, and both earth bank and hedge shielding at the trackside. A main road was reduced from six to four lanes to provide space for the Stadtbahn. This simplified construction and saved money on bridge reconstruction over a canal, as well as providing a visual incentive for motorists to switch to public transport. The journey time for the 12 km from Leopoldshafen to Karlsruhe city centre is 26 minutes, with peak limited-stop services taking only 20 minutes. All bus services were rearranged to offer two or three minute connections with the Stadtbahn, and as the buses share the same

◀The Albtalbahn ticket machine at each stop is an expensive item from the Swiss firm of Autelca and permits passengers to choose anything from a single ride to the monthly 'environmental' pass. A notechanger is on the right-hand side. *M.R. Taplin*

▼Low platforms provide near-level access to the first step of the light rail cars. Station platforms are well lit and sheltered. *M.R. Taplin*

▲The suburban portion of the northern Hardtbahn runs through residential areas in a shallow cutting to minimise intrusion, with ramps and bridges at each stop. *M.R. Taplin*

radio communication frequency as the Stadtbahn these connections are guaranteed.

On 3 June 1989 the Hardtbahn was extended 4.3 km from Leopldshafen-Nord to Linkenheim and Hochstetten. The line is single track for 3.5 km with a crossing loop at Linkenheim (Friedrichstrasse) and is operated under railway regulations as far as Grenzstrasse, where the Stadtbahn becomes a double-track line operated on sight. The 2-km freight branch to the nuclear research centre was electrified later in 1989 to provide light rail service for the 5000 workers there and useful contra-flow traffic for the AVG at peak periods, as well as saving the operation of many buses which ran in convoy to the city centre.

▲The need to insert the light rail line between existing housing at Leopoldshafen brought the construction on these concrete and hedge barriers to eliminate any noise nuisance. *M.R. Taplin*

◀Light rail cars have the potential to exceed the speed limit on the adjacent highway by 10 km/h as they run from Leopoldshafen to Linkenheim. *M.R. Taplin*

Traffic calming in Linkenheim.

◀The main street has been cleared of through motor traffic and the light rail line with two-way traffic inserted on a marked alignment that can be crossed by cars. Kerbs have been removed and shrub/tree planting carried out. *M.R. Taplin*

◀▼Outside the Rathaus motor traffic is discouraged from using the light rail tracks at all. *M.R. Taplin*

Important considerations apply to the provision of suburban services outside the city boundary, especially when urban services are run at a loss. In the case of Karlsruhe, the annual deficit on the urban tram and bus services is about DM 32 million for about 60 million passengers; this represents about 30% of costs. AVG contributes an operating surplus of about DM 1 million per annum. It is important to provide good public transport between a city and its region, not only to reduce the possible drift of the population from the city into its environs, but also to reduce the risk of a flow of purchasing power from the city.

It is therefore important that proper understanding is reached between the city, the administrative region (Landkreis) and the regional towns and communities to be served, and the basis of this is an appropriate cost-sharing agreement. The first was the 1974 agreement between Karlsruhe and Karlsbad for the 9-km AVG extension to Ittersbach. It was followed in 1982 by a similar agreement with Eggenstein-Leopoldshafen for the extension of the Hardtbahn, and in 1986 with Rheinstetten for the 6-km Südbahn extension. Similar agreements were made with the communities in Bretten, Pfinztal and Wörth for the new services currently being built or planned, although in these cases the DB has also to be a party to the agreement.

The Karlsruher Strasse in Linkenheim is an excellent example of the traffic-calming techniques developed in West Germany, with the single-track Stadtbahn laid in the narrowed street, now partly a pedestrian zone. Access by motor vehicle is possible, but discouraged by signing and perceived barriers; traffic is limited to 30 km/h. Hochstetten terminus has a small depot, complete with inspection pit, giving covered accommodation for four Stadtbahn cars, with siding space for eight more, and permitting wasteful dead running to be eliminated for first and last cars. At present seven cars run out between 04.42 and 06.52.

Traffic on the Hardtbahn has increased sufficiently to justify an all-day 10-minute service to Neureut, a 20-minute service to Leopoldshafen (10-minutes at peaks) and a 30-minute service to Linkenheim–Hochstetten (20-minutes at peaks). 37% of traffic comes from Park-and-Ride.

The light rail stop at Linkenheim Rathaus features this shelter embracing ticket machine, litter bins, illuminated service information, clock, loudspeaker for announcements from control and bicycle parking facilities. *M.R. Taplin*

▲Intermediate stops are also well-equipped in an up-to-date style. Linkenheim–Friedrichstrasse shows the long crossing loop to minimise the potential for delays on the single-track line.
M.R. Taplin

As a general basis of the agreements, Karlsruhe city builds and operates a Stadtbahn service linking the communities with the city tramway system. The communities pay 15% of the capital cost, although the Landkreis would normally meet half of this. The communities meet the share of any operating deficit attributable to their passengers; in return they have a right to regulate the losses through their participation in setting the level of service and fare structure. The cost of new vehicles is divided equally between the city and communities. This ensures that Karlsruhe pays its share in respect of the city service and also obtains the benefit of reduced private motoring. The agreements are for 30 years, corresponding to the expected life of the vehicles.

LINKING TRAM AND TRAIN

The success of the Albtalbahn and Hardtbahn prompted a study into how other communities around Karlsruhe might benefit from similar regional light rail links into the city centre. In particular linking the light rail and DB systems could improve the modal split in favour of public transport by offering faster and more convenient journeys, complete with savings in energy use and reductions in atmospheric pollution. There are seven DB local services working in the area around Karlsruhe, where the DB station is on the edge of the central area and no through services are possible with the present layout, technology and institutional arrangements. The study identified two routes (Wörth and Bretten) where relatively straightforward links could be achieved, offering time savings of 12–13 minutes to the 60% of passengers with their origin or destination in the city centre.

Research was required into four aspects: construction work, vehicle technology, operation of services and economic considerations. The most important decision was the correct power system for the vehicles; the light rail system and urban tramway use 750 V dc supply and impose constraints on minimum curve radius (25 m) and vehicle width (2.65 m), while the vehicles must be able to operate on DB tracks electrified at 15 kV ac and on non-electrified tracks. Options considered for a two-system vehicle were: dc-ac supply with vehicle-mounted transformer and rectifier; dc supply and diesel generator; dc supply with energy store (if sodium-sulphur battery development progressed satisfactorily); dc supply and combined use of diesel generator with energy store (battery or flywheel). The most attractive option in terms of weight, cost and space considerations was the dc-ac supply, with dc supply and sodium-sulphur battery as a possible future option for non-electrified lines.

In 1987 an AVG Stadtbahn car was equipped with transformer and rectifer equipment on an experimental basis and ran 1000 km of trials on DB tracks around the Karlsruhe station area electrified at 15 kV ac. In view of its potential national application, the trial was financed by the Federal Ministry for Research and Technology. No fundamental technical difficulties were revealed, and it was clear that the extra space required by the dual-voltage equipment could be fitted below the centre section of an eight-axle Stadtbahn car without much reducing the passenger. The additional weight was 3.6 t and the additional cost DM 150 000. A further trial with battery power has still to take place as new battery technology has not progressed as quickly as was hoped.

After protracted negotiations with DB, the basic agreement on the construction, operation and financing of the 28.2-km Stadtbahn Karlsruhe–Bretten (including 23.8 km over DB tracks between Durlach and Bretten–Gölshausen) was signed on 8 November 1988. The arrangements are of both national and international interest, as for the first time a section of main-line railway, retaining railway passenger service, will be physically linked with a tramway system to provide a through service from the hinterland into a city centre worked by light rail vehicles. The agreement comprised nine sections, and its primary purpose was to ensure that a project costing DM 80 million (about £26 million) at 1987 prices was securely financed.

The signatories represented not only the city of Karlsruhe and DB, but also the Landkreis, the town of Bretten and the local authority of Walzbachtal. In each case the appropriate executive body had to approve the proposals before they could be signed. A further signatory was the representative of the Geschaftsbereich Bahnbus (GBB), the local bus undertaking formed from the merger of DB and Postbus operations.

To a large extent the Karlsruhe–Bretten line will use the available infrastructure of DB and VBK, but there is still a need for work costing DM 45 million, in six main categories:
(a) new link tracks, including ramp, platforms and turning circle at Durlach station;
(b) double-track Stadtbahn alongside DB tracks between Durlach and the junction for the Bretten line at Grötzingen;

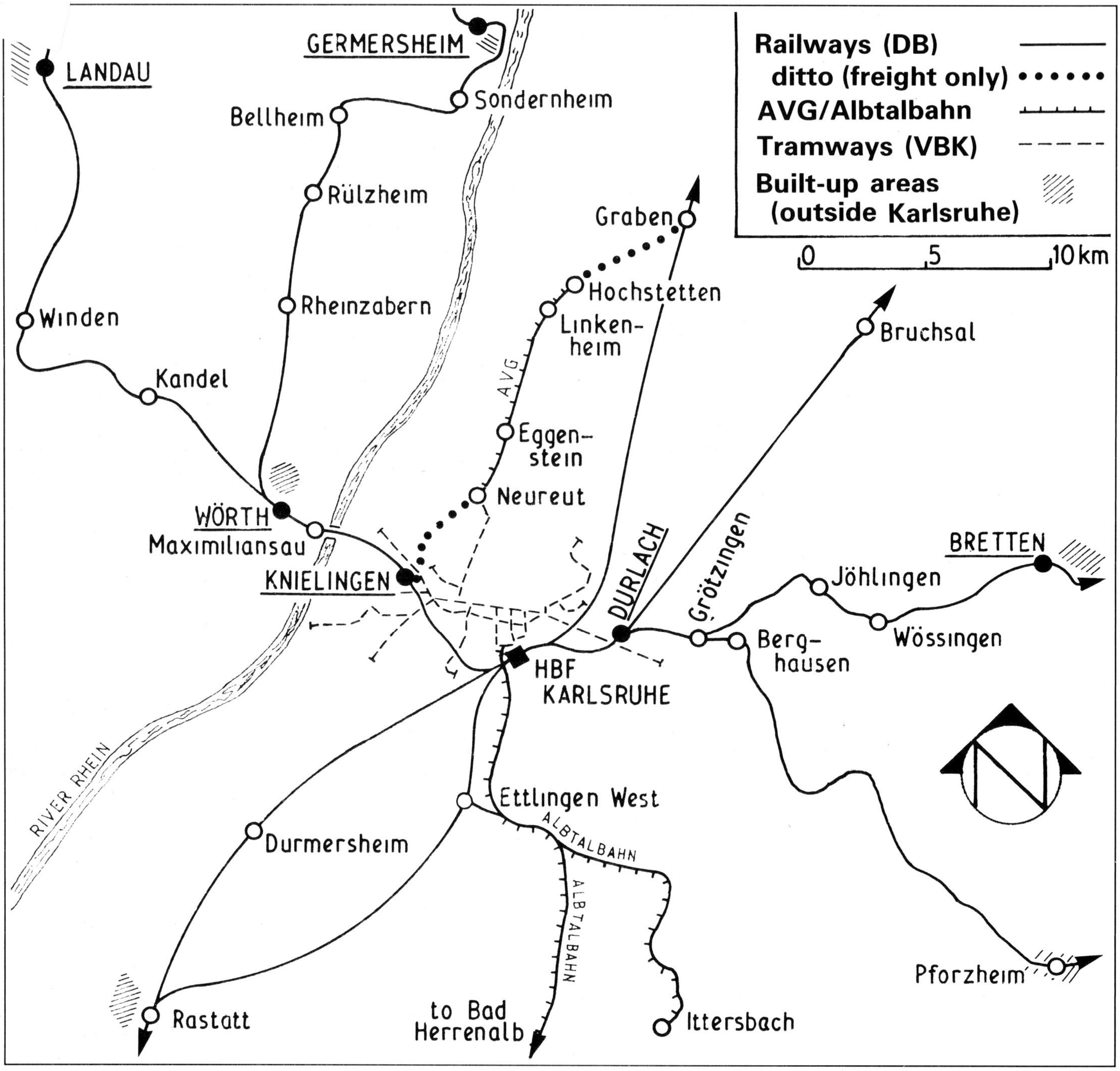

(c) electrification at 15 kV ac of the DB tracks from Grötzingen to Bretten;
(d) provision of a passing station between Grötzingen and Wössingen;
(e) provision of eight new halts along the existing line;
(f) improved access to stations in Jöhlingen and Wössingen.

In accordance with the Transport Financing Law for Local Communities, 85% of the cost will be met by the Federal Government and the Land of Baden–Württemberg. The balance of DM 6.75 million is divided as follows: city DM 2.18 M, Landkreis DM 2.285 million, Bretten DM 1.425 million and Walzbachtal DM 0.87 m.

The peak vehicle requirement for the Karlsruhe–Bretten service will be eight dual-voltage eight-axle Stadtbahn cars of type GT8-100C-2 (for 100 km/h operation with chopper control), but because of their innovative design as dual-voltage vehicles a total fleet of 10 cars is deemed advisable. The 10 cars were ordered from Duewag/ABB in December 1988 at a total cost of DM 35 million; with no Federal or Land subsidy available for vehicles, the city will bear the lion's share of DM 21 million, leaving the Landkreis to find DM 7.5 million, Bretten DM 4.45 million and Walzbachtal DM 2.05 million. Each car will be double-articulated, and unlike existing Stadtbahn cars, equipped for double-ended operation to be more suitable for running on the DB.

The line will have an hourly service (every 30 minutes at peaks). The Stadtbahn service will replace the present DB stopping trains, but the line will still be used by semi-fast trains from Karlsruhe to Heilbronn via Bretten. The present fare system of VBK and AVG will be extended to Bretten, and the new tickets will also be valid on the DB trains, so developing the fare system in the Karlsruhe area to match the classic Tarifverbünde in other major West German conurbations. Any deficit incurred by the Stadtbahn service will be borne by the city, Bretten and Walzbachtal in proportion to the passengers originating in their territory. As a consequence of this support, the authorities concerned will have a say in the quality of service and the fare structure.

Further regulations resolving major matters affecting the co-operating bodies cover the details of the joint service, the conditions under which Stadtbahn vehicles use DB facilities,

GBB bus services (with a new structure of feeder bus routes), the allocation of receipts and the questions of liability. By now the arrangements for the first section, the link at Durlach station, will have been completed and authorised. The second section from Durlach to Grötzingen is being worked on, while the arrangements for the section from Grötzingen to Bretten–Gölshausen concern only the DB. Project management is in the hands of VBK. Given no unforeseen problems or delays, service should begin in the second half of 1991.

OTHER DEVELOPMENTS

Karlsruhe's main shopping street is the Kaiserstrasse, running east-west through the city centre. The central 2 km from Hauptpost to Berliner Platz are reserved for pedestrians and trams, in contrast to many German cities, which have spent huge sums putting their tramways underground in city centres. Karlsruhe realised that burying public transport was not the best way to maximise its potential; the visible presence and surface boarding and alighting generate traffic and bring life to the city centre, a counter-attraction to sterile out-of-town shopping. At peak periods there is a tram every minute in each direction, including some multiple-unit operation and the Stadtbahn cars, yet accidents involving trams are very low: two accidents per million vehicle-km in pedestrian areas, and 80% of these are in-vehicle incidents. No buses are allowed into this part of Kaiserstrasse, although a few still run into less obvious parts of the city centre to connect with the trams.

Earlier efforts to serve the inner south-west suburb of Beiertheim by tram between the wars having achieved insufficient traffic, a major new initiative to serve a wider area was the extension of urban tram route 6 to Europahalle in 1983 and on to Oberreut in 1986. This last extension includes a long section on viaduct, including the 500-metre Bannwald bridge, and has been successful in meeting the public transport needs of this community.

On 29th May 1989 route 5 was extended by 0.95 km from its old terminus at Neureuterstrasse to Siemensallee, adjacent to the major Siemens complex. At a later date there will be a further extension with three stops along Siemensallee and Sudetenstrasse to Knielingen Nord, supplementing route 1 (which runs in Rheinbergstrasse) and turning 1.2 km beyond the present terminus. As it was not worth building a short-term loop at Siemensallee, cars still turn at Neureuterstrasse and run backwards to the new terminus using their rear-end supplementary controller, changing tracks at a crossover. The new section is double track on reservation, with two light-controlled crossings where trams have priority.

In addition to the Albtalbahn, there was a metre-gauge Lokalbahn in Karlsruhe that provided a cross-city electric service between Hagsfeld and Durmersheim, and was closed in 1937 after electrification in 1936! It is ironic that proposals for new tram services include the restoration of routes roughly serving the two ends of this former line. One concerns the extension from Rheinstrandsiedlung to Mörsch (a short distance from Durmersheim), then branching to Bach-West. The whole area from Forcheim to Mörsch and Bach-West has recently been incorporated within the boundaries of the town of Rheinstetten. Work on this 6.2 km Südbahn began in December 1988, and the first stage will run to the north side of Mörsch. An active debate has been opened about further extension, not only to Bach-West, but also to Bietigheim and the important town of Rastatt (which at present suffers from a poor train service to Karlsruhe).

At the north-east end of the former Lokalbahn was the never-electrified section from Hagsfeld to Spöck via Blankenloch. This area of the Stutensee local authority is taking great interest in having a Stadtbahn service. It might branch off route 4 at Sinsheimer Strasse, or could equally be served by an extension from the route 3 terminus at Rintheim. These are more recent developments of an earlier proposal to extend route 4 from Waldstadt to Europaschule.

The second Stadtbahn route from Karlsruhe to use DB passenger tracks will run initially to Wörth. The Wörth town council has approved the new link without a dissenting vote and a formal agreement modelled on the Bretten line example is imminent. This new link will branch from the city tramway at the Siemens stop on route 1 and run to the DB station at Knielingen. From here cars will run under DB overhead to Bf Wörth, where the Stadtbahn will branch away from DB tracks into the town, with seven new stops. The line will finish near the DB tracks on to Kandel and Landau, so making further extension over this line possible. In the meantime Bf Wörth will be the change point for passengers to and from Landau and Germersheim. An essential prerequisite to the construction of this line is a new Meccano-like single track bridge across the Rhein, which can be widened subsequently by plugging in extra parts to take a second track.

CONCLUSION

After building-up an effective a modern urban tramway system, within a few years Karlsruhe and its surrounding region will also have a completely integrated rail passenger network, achieved at relatively low cost and without massive civil engineering work or disruption. Light rail has been chosen in preference to buses because of its capacity, quality, environmental friendliness, and lower operating costs per passenger. The city shows how the modal split can be influenced in favour of public transport without resorting to draconian car restriction policies or road pricing.

STADTBAHN FLEET

Car type	GT6-80C	GT8-80C	GT8-100C2
Fleet numbers	501–545	581–585	not alloc.
Building dates	1983–89	1989–90	1990–1
Length overall (m)	27.6	38.4	37.6
Width overall (m)	2.65	2.65	2.65
Body height over rails (m)	3.4	3.4	3.4
Bogie wheelbase	2.1	2.1	2.1
Bogie centre separation (m)	10	13.8–9.77	13.4–9.77
Minimum curve radius (m)	23	25	25
Axle arrangement	B'2'B'	B'2'2'B'	B'2'2'B'
Weight unladen (t)	39.4	51	58
Maximum speed (km/h)	80	80	100
Seats	96	118+1	101+1
Standing (4/m^2)	89	124	124
Acceleration, max (m/s^2)	1.3	1.0	0.9
Braking, max service (m/s^2)	1.6	1.2	1.2
Braking, emergency (m/s^2)	3	3	3
Motor rating (kW)	2 x 280	2 x 245	2 x 245
Electrical supply	dc	dc	ac/dc
Air conditioning	No	Yes	No
Builders:	(501–520) Waggon Union-BBC (521–540) Duewag-BBC (others) Duewag-ABB	Duewag-ABB	Duewag-ABB

ACKNOWLEDGEMENTS

The author wishes to thank Dipl.-Ing. Georg Drechsler, Baudirektor of VBK and AVG, for source material, use has also been made of earlier English-language documentation prepared by VBK. Other references include:

Karlsruher Wirschaftspiegel, "In der Region Karlsruhe: Neue öffentliche Verkehrs-verbindungen".
Der Nahverkehr, "Stadtbahnbetrieb Karlsruhe auf ehmaliger Bundesbahnstrecke" by D. Ludwig and G. Drechsler; Der Stadtverkehr, issues 1/89 and 4/89.
ABB Traction, Stadtbahnwagen descriptive folders.
Blickpunkt Strassenbahn, 1988 and 1989 issues.
Modern Tramway 12/85, "Linking tram and train in Karlsruhe".
Avon County Council European Study Tour: Draft Report.

SYSTEM DESIGN

Safety of Light Rail Systems in the UK

by Peter Fox

INTRODUCTION

Railways in the UK are operated to a set of requirements issued by the Department of Transport known as the "Department of Transport Railway Construction and Operation Requirements". It is important to note that these requirements are not mandatory nor statutory, but since no railway can open unless cleared to do so by the Railway Inspectorate, failure to attain the standards contained therein would most likely lead the inspecting officer to recommend that the opening of the railway be postponed.

Technical standards for tramways were laid down in a memorandum issued in 1926, and certain of these standards were then incorporated into regulations made by the Minister of Transport for each individual undertaking.

With so many light rail schemes under consideration at present, the Railway Inspectorate have decided to include a section on LRT systems in the Construction and Operation Requirements which are at present being revised. In addition they have recently issued a provisional guidance note for the highway and vehicle engineering aspects of street running LRT systems.

THE GUIDANCE NOTE – GENERAL

It is important to note that LRT in this context means "light rapid transit" rather then "light rail transit" and is defined as "any guided transit system used for the carriage of passengers where the characteristics of the vehicles do not conform to those required for main line railways". Thus rubber-tyred or maglev systems are included as well as conventional light rail systems.

CATEGORIES OF LRT

For the first time categories are established for light rail systems as follows:

LRT1. The whole or part of an LRT system which runs in a road where the part of the carriageway used by the LRV is shared with other road users including pedestrians.

LRT2. The whole or part of an LRT system which runs in a road but where the LRT track is not shared, but is made accessible throughout its length for use by other road vehicles during traffic emergencies.

LRT3. The whole or part of an LRT system where the LRT tracks are wholly segregated from other road traffic, including pedestrians, either within the boundaries of a highway or in a totally separate alignment. This category may be subdivided into systems on which LRVs are operated:

(i) LRT3a on line of sight and will not require to be fully fenced;

(ii) LRT3b under the control of an interlocked signalling system and will normally be fully fenced.

Thus the traditional UK street tramway would be classed as LRT1, the current paved section on Blackpool Promenade as LRT2 and the Docklands Light Railway and Tyne & Wear Metro as LRT3b. Certain reserved sections between Blackpool & Fleetwood are LRT3a, and this category will be used extensively on the proposed Sheffield line 1.

AT GRADE LRT-ROAD INTERSECTIONS

On LRT1 and LRT2, road junctions are treated as normal road layouts, with the level of precendence being agreed with the highway authority. Additional warning signs need to be provided on the approches to, or junctions with, shared lanes.

On LRT3a, the intersections are treated like an intersection between two roads, but with priority given to LRT with signals and signs installed to ensure this.

On LRT3b, intersections are treated as level crossings, and therefore the appropriate type of crossing that would be used on a normal railway is specified, the type being dependant on the maximum speed of the LRT line, the frequency of road traffic and local visibility conditions.

LRT AND PEDESTRIANS

On LRT1 and on other systems where the LRT crossing cannot be separated from the crossing of the remainder of the highway, pedestrian crossings are operated so that any signal given to the LRT shows an aspect compatible with the aspect shown to the other highway users. This is known as *positive signalling*.

On systems where the crossing of the LRT tracks can be a self-contained part of the crossing movement and can be separated from other road users by refuges, a warning is only given when an LRV is approaching the crossing. This is known as *negative signalling*. A visible signal of twin flashing amber lights is given plus a distinctive audible warning.

Non-signalled crossings are also allowed where appropriate, and can include zebra and school crossings.

An interesting problem occurs when a junction is required to be co-located with a pedestrian crossing, or to be located where there could be problems for cyclists or motor cyclists. Pre-sorting is proposed in this case with interleaved track. A visual signal must be presented to the LRV driver showing the lie of the points.

SIGNS AND SIGNALS

Road signs already in existence for approaching electrified railways, and for rail/road crossings are used in connection with LRT routes, except that the picture of a train where provided would be replaced by a picture of a tram (preferably a more up-to-date design than that shown in the DTp document!). Similarly, exisiting signs for bus priorities are used, suitably modified with pictures of trams instead of buses. A new sign to inform pedestrians of the presence of a tramway is proposed (fig. 1).

In order to give instructions to LRV drivers which are not required to be observed by other road users, a new series of signs for erection on the highway is proposed. All are black on white, except the signs for indication of the stop position at a station which could be white on a coloured background, the colour not being white or pale yellow.

Special signals are required for LRVs so that their aspects cannot be confused with standard road traffic or railway lineside signals, although conventional railway signals would normally be used on LRT3b, and possibly on LRT3a. The signal would either be a multi-lamp (theatre-type) indicator showing an array of at least five white lights. Alternatively, a conventional three-aspect traffic signal may be used with suitable lenses to show white aspects (fig. 2). The signals may be located on the same post as the road traffic lights.

Fig. 1. The proposed sign to inform pedestrians of the presence of a tramway. The words "LEFT" or "RIGHT" may be substituted for "BOTH WAYS".

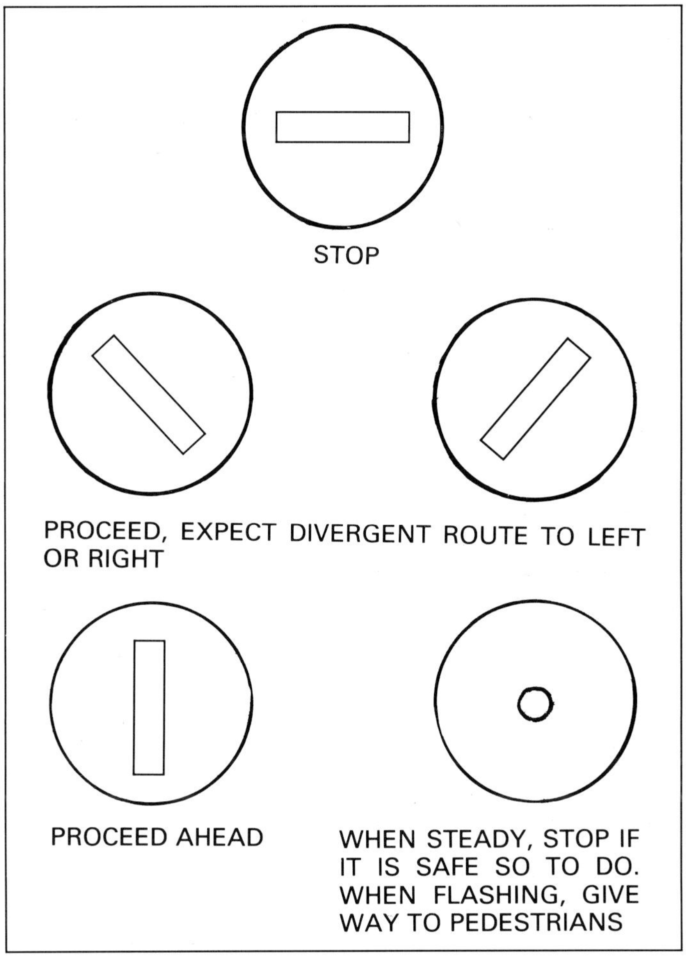

Fig. 2. Aspects to be displayed by LRT signals. All aspects are white.

▼Interleaved track in Basel, being used on a narrow section to avoid pointwork. In the UK it is proposed for pre-sorting at junctions. *John C. Baker*

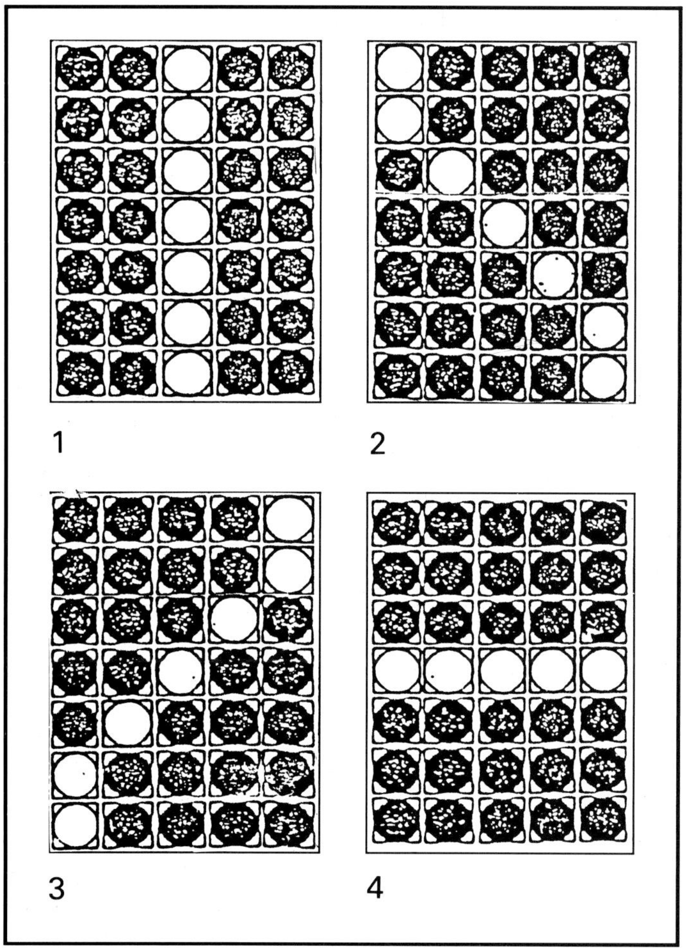

Fig. 3. An LRT dot matrix point indicator. The aspects are: (1) Points set for straight ahead. Proceed. (2 & 3) Points set for turnout to left or right. Proceed. (4) Points misaligned. Stop.

▲An LRV signal in Grenoble. The middle aspect is the equivalent of a yellow traffic light, whereas in the UK proposals this would mean "expect a route diverging to the right". *Peter Fox*

The LRV traffic signal will not be used to indicate the lie of a set of points. This will be done by a special indicator (fig. 3). However, it may indicate the route to be expected.

LRT signals which are associated with road traffic signals will be controlled by the local road signal controller. Any route information generated by the LRT system must be presented via a local LRT interface. Where the local control equipment is linked to a central controller, it must be able to function on its own if that link fails.

HIGHWAY AND CARRIAGEWAY DELINEATION

In pedestrian zones into which LRVs are permitted, the road surface in the swept path must be plainly identified by lines, or by differences in its colour and/or texture (see photo page 29). The *swept path* is determined as follows:

> The *Kinematic Envelope (KE)* is the line around the track in a plane normal to the track which encloses the extreme position of the vehicle, under all conditions of its movement, on straight and level track. The KE takes account of suspension movement, wear, tolerances in manufacture and the effects of tolerances in line, level and gauge of the track. It is speed dependant.
>
> The *Developed Kinematic Envelope (DKE)* is the KE enlarged to take into account all the possible effects of curvature, including superelevation of the track and end and centre throw of the vehicle. It is *unique to the particular location at a given speed.*
>
> The *Swept Path* is the DKE enlarged to take account of the required clearance outside the LRT track or tracks. The edge of the swept path is at least 280 mm outside the DKE.

The above considerations lead to a lane shared with other traffic on a single carriageway being at least 3.53 m wide for a 2.65 m-wide LRV. Where there are two or more lanes in a single direction and the LRT lane is shared with HGVs or PSVs then the minimum lane width is 3.3 m but the preferred width is 3.65 m.

The reserved track for LRT2 needs more than simple lining out to separate it from other lanes. A height difference of at least 150 mm is suggested, but suitable accesses must be provided for emergency vehicles or buses substituting for LRVs.

Finally, special provision may have to be made for cyclists and frontagers. When the LRT lane is at the side of the carriageway, a special mandatory cycle track is suggested. Similarly, arrangements have to be made for loading/unloading and parking to prevent the track being obstructed by road vehicles.

STATIONS

The transition between "high" and "low" platforms is defined as being 350 mm above the level of the track or carriageway. Most of the regulations concerned with stations are fairly obvious ones, e.g. the platform to be as long as the longest train to use it (with an extra allowance made for manual stopping) and fencing or steps to be provided to separate a high platform from normal pedestrian flows. Particular attention is paid in the regulations for access for the mobility-impaired; thus the regulations state that level transfer from the platform to the floor of the LRV must be provided through at least one door, and if access is via a ramp, then the ramp should preferably not be steeper than 1 in 20 and must not be steeper than 1 in 12. The 'level transfer' provision is to be welcomed, but one wonders why this applies only to LRT and not new stations on main-line railway systems.

◀A close up view of the bogie of a Grenoble LRV shows the skirting around the bogie which is required for safety purposes. Note also the magnetic track brakes. *Peter Fox*

OVERHEAD LINE EQUIPMENT

The maximum voltage allowed on LRT1 and LRT2 is 750, but on LRT3 1500 V may be used. Clearances are those for main-line railways, the wire height above the carriageway being 5.5 m. Previously this was 6.1 m and this means that special arrangements will be necessary on DTp high load routes.

VEHICLES

The following is a list of the more important features of LRVs which may be used on the highway:

- Normal road vehicle lighting plus amber marker lights and repeater direction indicators at intervals along the body sides.In additon a high intensity railway headlamp may be required for LRT3 sections.
- Any drawbar/coupler gear when out of use must not protrude beyond the vehicle ends, which must be protected by suitable fenders.
- The ends and sides of LRVs must be skirted to prevent, as far as is reasonably practicable, access to the underside of the vehicles. Skirts should be arranged to deflect anything which may come into inadvertent contact with the LRV.
- Normal service brakes should give a performance similar to that of PSVs.

The revision of the Railway Construction & Operation Requirements is yet to be issued, and this will contain the full description of features which must be built into an LRV.

INTER-WORKING

One topic which it is hoped that the revised Construction & Operation Requirements will address is that of the inter-working of LRT and conventional railways. The possibility of LRVs sharing tracks with conventional trains has generally been considered to be a non-starter, because of the DTp's insistence on a 150-tonne buffing load capability for normal rail vehicles. It has been argued that the LRV would also have to meet that requirement – very difficult in view of the fact that LRV floor height is invariably lower than that of conventional rail vehicles. As there are situations in the UK where a 25 kV ac electrified railway line could beneficially be integrated into an LRT system, a solution is required. to this problem.

It is considered that the solution to the problem lies in the fitting of ATP (automatic train protection) on the lines concerned. If the consequences of a conventional train hitting an LRV are thought to be unacceptably dangerous, then the solution is surely not to strengthen the LRV, but to ensure that the two different types of vehicle never come into contact. ATP ensures that, in the event of driver error, the train or LRV will stop automatically *before* a signal set at danger. The *Indusi* system used by the DB ensures the safety of the LRVs in the Karlsruhe area, and it is hoped that the new DTp requirements will allow similar interworking in the UK.

REFERENCES

(1) Tramways and Light Railways laid on Public Roads; memorandum regarding details of construction of new lines and equipment. Ministry of Transport 1926.
(2) The Department of Transport's Railway Construction and Operation Requirements. Published by HMSO in 1950 with later sections on Structural and Electrical Clearances (1977) and Level Crossings (1981 and 1985).
(3) Provisional Guidance Note on the Highway and Vehicle Engineering Aspects of Street-Running Light Rapid Transit Systems. Published by the Railway Inspectorate, Department of Transport, April 1989.
(4) Major C.B. Holden. Regulatory Requirements. Paper presented to the Institution of Electrical Engineers Colloquim "Light Rapid Transit on Street". 16th May 1989.

WORLD LIST

Urban Tramway and Light Rail Systems, 1990

by Michael Taplin

Note: This list excludes museums, rural and purely interurban lines.

* System built new since 1978.
§ System extending or extended recently, including subway construction.
† System with no light rail features.
(T) Heritage tramway operated primarily for tourist purposes.

Systems in italics are steel wheel, automated, fully-segregated lines

ARGENTINA

Buenos Aires*.

AUSTRALIA

Adelaide, Bendigo(T), Melbourne§.

AUSTRIA

Gmunden, Graz, Innsbruck, Linz§, Wien (Vienna)§.

BELGIUM

Antwerpen§, Bruxelles/Brussel (Brussels)§, Charleroi§, Gent§, Oostende.

BRAZIL

Campos do Jordao, Rio de Janeiro* (also T).

BULGARIA

Sofia§.

CANADA

Calgary*, Edmonton*, Toronto§, *Vancouver**.

CHINA

Anshan, Changchun, Dalian.

CZECHOSLOVAKIA

Bratislava§, Brno§, Kosice, Liberec, Most, Olomouc, Ostrava, Plzen§, Praha (Prague)§, Teplice-Trencianska.

EGYPT

El Qahira (Cairo), Helwan*, Iskandariyah (Alexandria), Masr-el-Gedida (Heliopolis).

FINLAND

Helsinki§.

FRANCE

Grenoble*, Lille, Marseille, Nantes*, St Etienne§.

GERMANY (DDR)

Bad Schandau(T), Berlin (East)§, Brandenburg§, Cottbus§, Dessau§, Dresden§, Erfurt§, Frankfurt/Oder§, Gera§, Görlitz§, Gotha, Halberstadt†, Halle§, Jena†, Karl-Marx-Stadt§, Leipzig, Magdeburg, Naumburg†, Nordhausen†, Plauen§, Potsdam§, Rostock§, Schöneiche, Schwerin§, Strausberg, Woltersdorf†, Zwickau§.

GERMANY (BRD)

Augsburg, Bielefeld§, Bochum-Gelsenkirchen§, Bonn, Braunschweig§, Bremen, Darmstadt, Dortmund§, Duisburg§, Düsseldorf§, Essen§, Frankfurt/Main§, Freiburg/Breisgau§, Hannover§, Heidelburg§, Karlsruhe§, Kassel§, Köln (Cologne)§, Krefeld§, Ludwigshafen, Mainz§, Mannheim, Mülheim/Ruhr§, München (Munich), Nürnberg, Stuttgart§, Ulm, Würzburg§.

HONG KONG

Hong Kong†, Tuen Men*.

HUNGARY

Budapest§, Debrecen†, Miskolc†, Szeged†.

INDIA

Calcutta§.

ITALY

Milano§, Napoli§, Roma§, Torino§.

JAPAN

Enoshima, Fukui, Gifu, Hakodate, Hiroshima, Kagoshima, Kitakyushu, Kochi, Kuamamonto, Kyoto, Matsuyama, Nagasaki, Okayama, Osaka, Sapporo, Takaoka, Tokyo, Toyama, Toyohashi.

MEXICO

Guadalajara*, Mexico City§.

NETHERLANDS

Amsterdam§, Den Haag (The Hague)§, Rotterdam§, Utrecht*.

NORWAY

Oslo.

PARAGUAY

Asuncion†.

PHILLIPINES

Manila*.

POLAND

Bydgoszcz§, Czestochowa, Elblag§, Gdansk (Danzig)§, Grudziadz, Katowice, Krakow, Lodz, Poznan, Szczecin (Stettin), Torun§, Warszawa (Warsaw)§, Wroclaw (Breslau).

PORTUGAL

Lisboa†, Porto†.

ROMANIA

Arad§, Braila, Brasov*, Bucuresti§, Cluj*, Constanta*, Craiova*, Galati§, Iasi§, Oradea§, Ploeisti*, Resita*, Sibiu†, Timisoara§.

SPAIN

Barcelona(T), Soller(T), Valencia*.

SWEDEN

Göteborg (Gothenburg)§, Lidingö, Norrköping§.

SWITZERLAND

Basel§, Bern, Bex†, Genève§, Neuchâtel, Zürich§.

TUNISIA

Tunis*.

TURKEY

Istanbul*, Konya*.

UNITED KINGDOM

Blackpool, Douglas(T), *London**, Newcastle-upon-Tyne*.

UNITED STATES

Boston, Buffalo*, Cleveland, Dallas(T), *Detroit** (also T), Fort Worth, Galveston(T), Newark, New Orleans (also T), Philadelphia, Pittsburgh§, Portland*, Sacramento*, San Diego*, San Francisco§, San Jose*, Seattle(T).

USSR

(§† information not available).

Achinsk, Alma Ata, Angarsk, Arkhangelsk, Astrakhan, Avdeyevka, Baku, Barnaul, Biysk, Chelyabinsk, Cherepovets, Daugavpils, Dneprodzerzhinsk, Dnepropetrovsk, Donetsk, Druzhkovka, Dzerzhinsk, Gorki, Gorlovka, Grozniy, Irkutsk, Ivanovo, Kalinin, Kaliningrad, Karaganda, Karpinsk, Kazan, Kemerovo, Khabarovsk, Kharkov, Kiev, Kolomna, Komsomolsk, Konotop, Konstantinovka, Kramatorsk, Krasnoarmeisk*, Krasnodar, Krasnoturinsk, Krasnoyarsk, Krivoy Rog, Kuibyshev, Kursk, Kuznetsk, Leningrad, Liepaya, Lipetsk, Lvov, Magnitogorsk, Makeyevka, Minsk, Moskva (Moscow), Mosyr*, Naberezhyne-Chelny, Nikolayev, Nishnikamensk, Nishni Tagil, Noginsk, Novocherkassk, Novopolotsk, Novosibirsk, Novotroisk, Odessa, Omsk, Orzhonikidze, Orel, Orsk, Ossinniki, Pavlodar, Perm, Prokopyevsk, Pyatigorsk, Riga, Rostov-na-Donu, Ryazan, Salavat, Saratov, Shakhty, Shushenskoye, Smolensk, Stakhanov, Stary Oskol*, Sumgait, Sverdlovsk, Taganrog, Tallinn, Tashkent, Tbilisi, Termitau, Tomsk, Tula, Ufa, Ulan Ude, Ulyanovsk, Ussolye-Sibiriskoye, Ust-Ilimsk*, Ustinov, Ust-Kamenogorsk, Vinnitsa, Vitebsk, Vladivostock, Volgograd, Volzhskiy, Volchansk, Voronezh, Voroshilovgrad, Yaroslavl, Yenakievo, Yerevan, Yevpatoria, Zaporozhye, Zhdanov, Zhitomir, Zlatoust.

VIETNAM

Hanoi†.

YUGOSLAVIA

Beograd§, Osijek, Sarajevo, Zagreb§.

SYSTEMS UNDER CONSTRUCTION

BRAZIL: Salvador.
FRANCE: Paris.
ITALY: Genova.
MEXICO: Monterrey.
SWITZERLAND: Lausanne.
UK: Manchester.
USA: Baltimore, Los Angeles, St Louis.
USSR: Togliatti.

SYSTEMS AUTHORISED

BRAZIL: Goiana, Teresina, Belo Horizonte.
CZECHOSLOVAKIA: Chomutov.
MALAYSIA: Kuala Lumpur.
SWEDEN: Stockholm(T).
UK: Bristol, Sheffield.
USA: Dallas, Denver, Houston, Minneapolis, Jersey City.

SYSTEMS PLANNED

These include:

ARGENTINA Cordoba.
AUSTRALIA Brisbane(T).
AUSTRIA Salzburg.
BRAZIL Brasilia.
COLOMBIA Bogota.
FRANCE Brest, Reims, Rouen, Strasbourg.
ITALY Bologna, Firenze.
NEW ZEALAND Auckland.
SPAIN Barcelona.
UK Birmingham.
USA Chicago, Norfolk, Phoenix, Seattle.

▼In Egypt tramway systems installed under European administration have been modernised and expanded to carry the burgeoning traffic in an environment where the average life of a bus is only two or three years. This is the interchange between the city tramways and Ramlen light rail line in Alexandria.
J.M. Moerland

A FALSE DAWN

Some Light Rail Developments 60 Years Ago

by Geoffrey Skelsey

One of the distinctive features of light rail transit (LRT), amongst innovative forms of urban public transport, is its long and progressive history of technical refinement. Compared with less orthodox systems, LRT offers a well-established, fully-tested technology with decades of diverse and effective development behind it.

The history of LRT is not simply a matter of nostalgia or antiquarian interest, although the vast and growing library of historical publications shows how important a part in our heritage was played by its direct antecedent, the street tramway. More important in the present context, is the fact that over a century of progress has produced effective and reliable answers to many of the problems likely to be encountered by the new generation of light rail promoters.

Trackwork, current supply and collection, suspension and running gear, control and traction equipment, body design: all these are areas in which the growing sophistication of the mode helps new installations to move smoothly and effectively towards successful operation. LRT is, above all, a predictable, realisable mode.

By contrast, unconventional systems inevitably involve a measure of experimentation, with all the implications in terms of uncertain costing and performance. Many systems are linked to proprietorial and patent interests which confine the sourcing of equipment and limit freedom to adapt and develop to meet individual local circumstances. Light rail, in short, is a tried, tested and mature technology, but one which has far from reached the limit of its potential development, and is available competitively from a variety of suppliers.

This article will mention briefly some of the ways in which technical refinement was achieved in the first phase of tramway development. In the space available there can only be a sketch of some of the main innovations, and the account is by no means comprehensive.

Several significant innovations occured in the 1920s, some exactly 60 years ago. For instance the gradual separation of trams from motorised traffic through the adoption of reserved tracks was introduced on the more progressive installations from the mid-1920s onwards, a notable example being the Bristol Road routes south of Birmingham, with about 10 km constructed on attractive tree-lined right-of-way in 1923–6. Although replaced by orthodox diesel bus services in 1952, these routes continue to handle very heavy traffic, and have been proposed as possible candidates for new LRT in due course as part of Midland Metro.

A more definite LRT revival concerned the York Road routes east of Leeds, a largely segregated installation of similar extent opened in 1924–36. These lines were included in the light rail plans for Leeds developed by the West Yorkshire Passenger Transport Executive in 1987–88; although the concept failed to find favour with the City Council, which is currently being seduced by promoters of proprietory automatic mini-metros, it is still realistic and could be reconsidered.

Projects such as these, in their original incarnation, produced solid experience in such fields as track foundations and geometry, and although for complex politico-economic reasons tramway development in Great Britain virtually ended 40 years ago (the last conventional extensions, in Glasgow, Leeds and Sunderland, all opened in 1949), progress continued apace in continental Europe and is now at the disposal of today's developers.

Then take lightweight vehicle construction, improved performance, and carefully researched body design. 1929 saw very important developments in this sphere, in both Great Britain and the United States. In London the first results were seen that year of the unique experimental programme carried out by the capital's company-owned suburban tramways. This research spawned three prototype cars that led directly to what were probably the country's most innovative tramcars, the UCC or Feltham trams (so named from their place of construction), of which 103 eventually ran in London, 92 of them surviving to go to Leeds in 1949–51, where they then ran until 1959 on the very routes described above.

Even in old age the technical features of these remarkable vehicles were ahead of their time. They included: passenger flow bodies with air-operated exit doors and special attention to the needs of standing passengers; lightweight construction, bringing down tare weight per passenger place, and minimising power consumption despite the very large size of the vehicles; special attention to crew and passenger comfort and amenities, including lighting and heating; and electrical and braking equipment of relative sophistication for the period.

For reasons of economy the 100 production vehicles lacked some refinements tried on the prototypes, such as aluminium body panels and equal-wheel monomotor trucks. But the Felthams were an outstanding achievement amongst British tramcar designs, although sadly they had little direct effect on an industry which was already becoming fossilized, even if no conventional service buses in fleet production matched them for 20 years or more.

Oddly enough, in the same year of 1929, the crucial first steps were taken in the United States to develop a standardised national tramcar, a design which was ultimately to have worldwide influence and to lead to the construction of more than 5000 units and four times that number of close copies. Many of the former and most of the latter are in service today, although almost all operate far from the country where the design was conceived. The Electric Railway Presidents' Conference Committee was established in Chicago late in 1929, with the specific duty of overseeing research, design and construction of a wholly-modern, state-of-the-art tramcar. A three-year research programme followed, costing (in modern currency values) some $US 20 million provided by 28 major American tramway operators and 26 car and equipment manufacturers.

Here at once was a major difference from the far more modest British project. In Great Britain most major operators built their own vehicles and, sadly, there was little industry-wide collaboration or consistent design standards (one explanation for the early decline of the British tramcar

▲After twenty years in London the Felthams found a new home in Leeds, where they still looked impressive in 1956. Elsewhere in the city there were fine modern private tracks to do justice to these outstanding trams. *the late R.B. Parr, courtesy Tramway Museum Society*

▼The longevity of the American PCC car is a tribute to its sound and advanced design. This 1951 example is one of many that Toronto refurbished in the 1970s for another 15 years service. *J.F. Bromley*

industry). The legendary PCC car was introduced in Brooklyn in 1934, and by the time the last rolled off the lines, for San Francisco in 1952, nearly 5000 had been built new for 28 North American cities. There were, however, many licensed overseas derivatives, notably from Belgium and Czechoslovakia, which still produce designs with PCC features today, so advanced were the concepts.

The PCC programme had something in common with the London experiments, despite the far smaller scale of the latter. Indeed the instruction given in London to the Feltham design team was almost identical to that specified in Chicago: every single tramcar component was to be re-examined and, where necessary, redesigned. Both projects paid particular attention to passenger amenity, acceleration, and reliable and smooth riding and braking, all vital considerations at a time of growing competition from both public and private motor transport. The greater resources devoted to the American project bore fruit in a far more advanced design, and one which had the considerable merit of adaptability to the individual constraints and requirements of different operators. The adoption of modular vehicle design meant that the basic car was capable of extensive variation, while retaining the advantage of lower unit costs, which favoured small orders.

There were three other outstanding features of the PCC. Firstly body design, fittings and door layout were planned to maximise passenger convenience and comfort, including the needs of standees. Such commonplace subjects as lighting, ventilation, and seat design were the subject of extended practical experiment on a scale probably never seen before in relation to urban vehicles. Secondly the PCC's electrical control system was a masterpiece of early control engineering, designed with some success to produce jerk-free and rapid acceleration and braking. And thirdly, wheels, trucks and gearing were completely redesigned to minimise noise and maximise ride quality. Many ERPCC patents covered wheel and truck design, in particular the use of rubber, and continue to influence present-day light rail vehicle design. Whilst such experiments were not unique (one thinks for instance of contemporary efforts by other American manufacturers, and the research leading to the Swiss standard tramcar of 1941), these were unparalleled at that time for comprehensiveness, and above all, effort.

In many respects both Felthams and PCCs came too late to have the impact they might have had in their own countries. The Felthams ran for less than a decade on the lines for which they were built, and the ideal of a new reserved track tramway to Uxbridge, which had been in the minds of their designers, was overtaken by the rapid change in policy in 1933 which sought to remove tramcars from London within a decade. In the USA half the sponsoring undertakings which financed the PCC research programme never bought a production unit, and the diminishing fleet of cars was shuffled in its later years from undertaking to undertaking (so that even in 1989 San Francisco is thinking of acquiring 20 PCCs from Philadelphia). In retrospect perhaps neither development exploited to the full the intrinsic merits of rail traction, and both were too similar in capacity and performance to the maturing motor bus to offer the decisive operational and economic advantages which elsewhere secured the retention of street-based rail transport.

In Great Britain the strangest anomaly was the continued attachment to double-deck vehicles. The merits of this were clear enough in terms of maximising seating capacity in relation to road space used, but the cost was relatively low total capacity and operational inflexibility, which particularly penalized the rail vehicle. There were isolated experiments with single-deck vehicles. Motor-and-trailer sets operated in Birmingham for a time, and later in Liverpool, in both of which cities subway construction was actively considered. There were similar experiments in Glasgow, Bradford and (at the last minute in 1953) Leeds, but none came to anything, for reasons that had very little to do with the merits of the experiments concerned. Otherwise, by persisting with the orthodox double decker the operators failed to benefit from major real and potential benefits of rail traction.

Staff/passenger ratios remained unfavourable. The use of obsolete or little-used railway rights of way as a lower cost means of achieving segregated routes was largely out of the question because of bridge heights. And the local use of underpasses or short subways to avoid conflict with other traffic was expensive and difficult. The better utilisation of staff and the reuse of rail routes is central to many of today's LRT developments in Great Britain. Current plans in Manchester, Bristol and the West Midlands all feature the incorporation of existing railway alignments into new light rail lines, but this is not in fact a new development. Again in 1929, the railway from Adelaide to Glenelg in South Australia was converted from ordinary steam trains to a high-speed electric tramway, using coupled single-deck cars which still run today. Interestingly, on the same continent, the latest extensions to the huge Melbourne tramway are light rail lines making use of a number of the city's suburban railways. It is significant that both these undertakings settled on single-deck operation at an early stage. Other similar developments occurred in North America, notably the conversion of a former canal routeway into a light rail line in Newark, New Jersey in 1935, and the conversion of Boston's Riverside railway to light rail in 1959. Both continue in use today.

Not until the German developments after about 1957 did the economics and operational characteristics of the orthodox tramway move decisively into the light rail era. The German car-design tradition was quite different both from the British practice of low-capacity, mainly-seated vehicles, and from the American PCCs with their high standard of comfort and sophisticated and expensive power control systems. The Germans maximised passenger capacity, provided for multiple-unit operation, stressed segregated tracks, and retained simple and robust control equipment (at least until the advent of power electronics). Theirs was, in the end, a tradition which adapted better to rapid transit operation, and it is no co-incidence that in the leading cities of the light rail revival, Newcastle-upon-Tyne, Edmonton and San Diego, it is essentially German designs and experience which underlie the system characteristics and the new generation of light rail vehicles.

The lessons of the last 60 years of light rail progress are simple though. Painstaking attention to passenger amenity improves LRT's competitive position. Standardisation and interchangeability of equipment produces crucial economies. And building on an established technological base speeds design, construction and effective operation. The developments of the 1920s and 1930s may have been a false dawn, but they helped to prepare for the real one.